When We Forgive, We Perform a Miracle Hardly Anyone Notices

We do it alone—in the private place of our inner selves.

We do it silently—no one can record our miracle on tape.

We do it invisibly—no one can record our miracle on film.

We do it freely—no one can ever trick us into forgiving someone.

But when we forgive, we heal the hurt we never deserved.

Forgive & Forget

FORGIVE & FORGET

Healing The Hurts We Don't Deserve

Lewis B. Smedes

PUBLISHED BY POCKET BOOKS NEW YORK

POCKET BOOKS, a division of Simon & Schuster, Inc.
1230 Avenue of the Americas, New York, N.Y. 10020

Published by arrangement with Harper & Row Publishers, Inc.
Library of Congress Catalog Card Number: 84-47736

ISBN: 0-671-60711-1

First Pocket Books printing March, 1986

10 9 8 7 6 5 4 3 2 1

POCKET and colophon are registered trademarks
of Simon & Schuster, Inc.

Printed in the U.S.A.

TO
my sister Jessie
and
my brother Peter
"letters written not by hand, but by the Spirit"

Contents

A Word of Thanks

I learned about forgiving, not by reading good books, but by listening to good forgivers. Several of them appear in this volume, most behind names not their own. I thank them for sharing their struggles and their triumphs with me.

I must also mention Dr. Paul Clement, who let me teach a seminar on forgiving with him at the Fuller Graduate School of Psychology and Dr. Carol Visser, who invited me to teach a workshop on the subject sponsored by the Creative Counseling Center in Hollywood. To Jan Gathright, who with patient grace and imaginative skills converted my wretchedly scribbled drafts into flawless script, I owe much of any merit this book may have in style and clarity. To my two editors, Linda Mead of L. T. Mead & Associates and Roy M. Carlisle of Harper & Row San Francisco, who taught me more about how to write a book than I thought I needed to know, I can only say thanks for teaching me so much so fast. My wife, Doris, on the other hand, taught me a love that makes forgiving possible, and I thank her from my heart.

I wrote much of the book while I was a fellow at the Institute for Ecumenical and Cultural Research, Collegeville, Minnesota, during the fall of 1983. I could not have found anywhere a setting more pleasant and conducive to remembering and writing; so I want to thank the trustees and, in particular, Robert Bilheimer, the director of the Institute, for their hospitality to me. The trustees of Fuller Seminary generously gave me sabbatical leave to make my visit possible, and I thank them.

I must tell you, too, that I would know little about our human faculty for forgiving had I not also felt Christ's gift of forgiving love in my own life; so I thank God for inventing the way to heal the hurts we don't deserve.

An Invitation

Somebody hurt you, maybe yesterday, maybe a lifetime ago, and you cannot forget it. You did not deserve the hurt. It went deep, deep enough to lodge itself in your memory. And it keeps on hurting you now.

You are not alone. We all muddle our way through a world where even well-meaning people hurt each other. When we invest ourselves in deep personal relationships, we open our souls to the wounds of another's disloyalty or even betrayal.

There are some hurts that we can all ignore. Not every slight sticks with us, thank God. But some old pains do not wash out so easily; they remain like stubborn stains in the fabric of our own memory.

Deep hurts we never deserved flow from a dead past into our living present. A friend betrays us; a parent abuses us; a spouse leaves us in the cold—these hurts do not heal with the coming of the sun.

We've all wished at one time or other that we could reach back to a painful moment and cut it out of our lives. Some people are lucky; they seem to have gracious glands that secrete the juices of forgetfulness. They never hold a grudge; they do not remember old hurts. Their painful yesterdays die with the coming of tomorrow. But most of us find that the pains of our past keep rolling through our memories, and there's nothing we can do to stop the flow.

Nothing?

The great Jewish philosopher Hannah Arendt, toward the end of her epochal study on *The Human Condition,* shared her discovery of the only power that can stop the inexorable stream of painful memories: the "faculty of forgiveness." It is as simple as that.

Forgiveness is God's invention for coming to terms with a world in which, despite their best intentions, people are unfair to each other and hurt each other deeply. He began by forgiving us. And he invites us all to forgive each other.

Virtually every newspaper in the Western world told the story of how, one January dawn in 1984, Pope John Paul walked into a dank cell of Rebibbia prison in Rome to meet Mehmet Ali Agca, the man who had tried to kill him. The Pope took the hand of the man who had fired a bullet at his heart, and forgave him.

But the Pope is a professional forgiver; and it may be easy for such a highly placed professional to forgive when he knows ahead of time that the whole world will be watching.

It is ten times harder for an ordinary person, whom nobody is watching, to forgive and forget.

Forgiving is love's toughest work, and love's biggest risk. If you twist it into something it was never meant to be, it can make you a doormat or an insufferable manipulator.

Forgiving seems almost unnatural. Our sense of fairness tells us people should pay for the wrong they do. But forgiving is love's power to break nature's rule.

Ask yourself these questions: What do I do when I forgive someone who has done me wrong?

Who is forgivable? Have some people gone beyond the forgiveness zone?

How do I do it?

Why should I even try? Is there a pay-off? Is it fair?

I invite you to come with me in search of the answers I have found along my own journey.

The Magic Eyes
A Little Fable

In the village of Faken in innermost Friesland there lived a long thin baker named Fouke, a righteous man, with a long thin chin and a long thin nose. Fouke was so upright that he seemed to spray righteousness from his thin lips over everyone who came near him; so the people of Faken preferred to stay away.

Fouke's wife, Hilda, was short and round, her arms were round, her bosom was round, her rump was round. Hilda did not keep people at bay with righteousness; her soft roundness seemed to invite them instead to come close to her in order to share the warm cheer of her open heart.

Hilda respected her righteous husband, and loved him too, as much as he allowed her; but her heart ached for something more from him than his worthy righteousness.

And there, in the bed of her need, lay the seed of sadness.

One morning, having worked since dawn to knead his dough for the ovens, Fouke came home and found a stranger in his bedroom lying on Hilda's round bosom.

Hilda's adultery soon became the talk of the tavern and the scandal of the Faken congregation. Everyone assumed that Fouke would cast Hilda out of his house, so righteous was he. But he surprised everyone by keeping Hilda as his wife, saying he forgave her as the Good Book said he should.

13

In his heart of hearts, however, Fouke could not forgive Hilda for bringing shame to his name. Whenever he thought about her, his feelings toward her were angry and hard; he despised her as if she were a common whore. When it came right down to it, he hated her for betraying him after he had been so good and so faithful a husband to her.

He only pretended to forgive Hilda so that he could punish her with his righteous mercy.

But Fouke's fakery did not sit well in heaven.

So each time that Fouke would feel his secret hate toward Hilda, an angel came to him and dropped a small pebble, hardly the size of a shirt button, into Fouke's heart. Each time a pebble dropped, Fouke would feel a stab of pain like the pain he felt the moment he came on Hilda feeding her hungry heart from a stranger's larder.

Thus he hated her the more; his hate brought him pain and his pain made him hate.

The pebbles multiplied. And Fouke's heart grew very heavy with the weight of them, so heavy that the top half of his body bent forward so far that he had to strain his neck upward in order to see straight ahead. Weary with hurt, Fouke began to wish he were dead.

The angel who dropped the pebbles into his heart came to Fouke one night and told him how he could be healed of his hurt.

There was one remedy, he said, only one, for the hurt of a wounded heart. Fouke would need the miracle of the magic eyes. He would need eyes that could look back to the beginning of his hurt and see his Hilda, not as a wife who betrayed him, but as a weak woman who needed him. Only a new way of looking at things through the magic eyes could heal the hurt flowing from the wounds of yesterday.

Fouke protested. "Nothing can change the past," he said. "Hilda is guilty, a fact that not even an angel can change."

"Yes, poor hurting man, you are right," the angel said. "You cannot change the past, you can only heal the hurt that comes to you from the past. And you can heal it only with the vision of the magic eyes."

"And how can I get your magic eyes?" pouted Fouke.

"Only ask, desiring as you ask, and they will be given you. And each time you see Hilda through your new eyes, one pebble will be lifted from your aching heart."

Fouke could not ask at once, for he had grown to love his hatred. But the pain of his heart finally drove him to want and to ask for the magic eyes that the angel had promised. So he asked. And the angel gave.

Soon Hilda began to change in front of Fouke's eyes, wonderfully and mysteriously. He began to see her as a needy woman who loved him instead of a wicked woman who betrayed him.

The angel kept his promise; he lifted the pebbles from Fouke's heart, one by one, though it took a long time to take them all away. Fouke gradually felt his heart grow lighter; he began to walk straight again, and somehow his nose and his chin seemed less thin and sharp than before. He invited Hilda to come into his heart again, and she came, and together they began again a journey into their second season of humble joy.

Part 1

THE FOUR STAGES OF FORGIVING

What do you do when you forgive someone who hurt you? What goes on? When is it necessary? What happens afterward? What should you expect it to do for you? *What is forgiving?*

The act of forgiving, by itself, is a wonderfully simple act; but it always happens inside a storm of complex emotions. It is the hardest trick in the whole bag of personal relationships.

So let us be honest with each other. Let us talk plainly about the "magic eyes" that are given to those who are ready to be set free from the prison of pain they never deserved.

We forgive in four stages. If we can travel through all four, we achieve the climax of reconciliation.

The first stage is *hurt:* when somebody causes you pain so deep and unfair that you cannot forget it, you are pushed into the first stage of the crisis of forgiving.

The second stage is *hate:* you cannot shake the memory of how much you were hurt, and you cannot wish your enemy well. You sometimes want the person who hurt you to suffer as you are suffering.

The third stage is *healing:* you are given the "magic eyes" to see the person who hurt you in a new light. Your memory is healed, you turn back the flow of pain and are free again.

The fourth stage is *the coming together:* you invite the person who hurt you back into your life; if he or she comes honestly, love can move you both toward a new and healed relationship. The fourth stage depends on the person you forgive as much as it depends on you; sometimes he doesn't come back and you have to be healed alone.

CHAPTER 1

We Hurt

If you live long enough, chances are you'll be hurt by someone you counted on to be your friend. If you're like me, you may let that hurt fester and grow until it stifles your joy. When that happens, you have entered the first stage of forgiving.

I'm talking about the kind of hurts that smart and rankle within us, the kind we cannot digest as if they were only so much fiber in our interpersonal diet. Our wounds may look superficial to others, but we know better; after all, we're the ones who feel them.

I'd like to tell you a little story about a hurt I felt once, to illustrate how something that may look insignificant to outsiders can push you into the crisis of forgiveness.

It's important, to begin with, to say that I come from a long line of village blacksmiths. In fact, our family name, Smedes, is an old Dutch word for smith. From the time people first took on surnames, every male child in our family grew up to earn his living pounding on an anvil, and it was a source of family pride to be a smith worthy of the vocation.

Now on to the story. I graduated, without distinction, from Muskegon Senior High School one June Friday night. The next day I rode a Greyhound bus to Detroit, where I began work in the yards of the Smedes Iron Works, a family-run shop that my Uncle Klass built up out of a smithy he operated in a garage in his early immigrant days. Because I had neither

19

money nor promising credentials for higher education, I was glad to accept Uncle Klass's offer to get my start in the steel business.

I was put to work out in the yard, rolling steel beams into neat stacks, cutting them with an acetylene torch into the sizes that building contractors ordered and painting them with a blend of gasoline and pitch to keep them from rusting too fast. I never did get to use the forge at which ornate forms were pounded and twisted out of red hot steel bars, the only genuine smithing still done at Smedes Iron Works.

To be honest, I was a sorry excuse for either a smith or a steelworker. I was too tall, too thin, too dreamy for any of the jobs that called for the blend of strength and talent it took to work with steel. No luster was added to the name of Smedes during my stint at the Iron Works.

My cousin Hank was different; he was born to the forge. His wrists were powerful, his hands were obedient to his mind, and he could see an artful form of steel in his mind's eye before he even put his hands to the hammer.

Hank sometimes took me along to construction sites, where we would install a gate or a fancy railing that he had crafted at the shop. He taught me how to chisel square holes into a concrete floor and set the gateposts in, pouring molten lead into the space left over. He occasionally took me into his confidence, telling me delicious family secrets about Uncle Klass and dirty jokes such as I had never heard before.

Gradually, Hank made me feel as if I were truly his friend.

But he seemed to have a dual personality. One side of him was friendly and fun; the other side was devious and cruel.

When he and I were alone, he showed me his friendly side. I accepted that part of him; it was certainly the only part that I needed.

But whenever somebody else came along while we were working—a building inspector, for instance—

Hank showed me his mean side. He turned on me, and always within earshot of the man who was watching us.

"Hey, Lew, get your skinny butt over here and do this job right for a change."

"This jackass they foisted on me as a helper doesn't know the difference between a hammer and a curling iron, but he's the boss's nephew so I have to put up with him."

"Lew, you ain't worth nothin' around here—you just better know that."

This is how Hank would talk to me, and about me, in front of the men we both wanted badly to impress as competent workmen.

He would set me up by getting me to believe that I was his friend; then he would humiliate me. I was a pushover, because at that time I needed a friend more than I needed anything else. So when Hank would show me his friendly side on our way home—even if he had made me feel like a fool that very day—I would fall for it, only to catch his scorn again the next day.

I hated Hank a lot, I suppose, and for a good while, too. And why shouldn't I have hated him? It hurts to be taken in as a friend and then treated like a stray dog. I knew in my heart that, even though I had set myself up as a sucker for the hurt Hank gave me, I didn't have it coming.

My hurt brought me into the first stage of forgiving—the critical stage at which I had to make a simple decision: Did I want to be healed, or did I want to go on suffering from an unfair hurt lodged in my memory?

We are always, all of us, pushed into this crucial stage when we feel that somebody has hurt us deeply. Will we let our pain hang on to our hearts where it will eat away our joy? Or will we use the miracle of forgiving to heal the hurt we didn't deserve?

Of course, we suffer a lot of superficial pains that nobody really needs to be forgiven for—mere indignities that we simply have to bear with a measure of grace.

21

We need to sort out our hurts and learn the difference between those that call for the miracle of forgiveness and those that can be borne with a sense of humor. If we lump all our hurts together and prescribe forgiveness for all of them, we turn the art of forgiving into something cheap and commonplace. Like good wine, forgiving must be preserved for the right occasion.

The hurt that creates a crisis of forgiving has three dimensions. It is always *personal, unfair,* and *deep*. When you feel this kind of three-dimensional pain, you have a wound that can be healed only by forgiving the one who wounded you.

PERSONAL PAIN

We can only forgive people, we cannot forgive nature, even though nature often hurts us. Sometimes the pain comes from what nature fails to give us— some people, through no fault of their own, are born into the world with less health, beauty, or intelligence than they want. Sometimes we simply reel from the assault of nature's fury, the way close friends of mine felt as they buried their baby the other day, a victim of the mystery called crib death. Each of us can be random victims of natural forces that strip us of our dignity and smash us without respect for merit or need.

But we cannot forgive nature. We can curse it, rage against it, blame it for all that is wrong with us, and finally surrender to its brute power. We can use science to defend ourselves temporarily against nature's whimsical savagery. Or, in faith, we can look beyond nature and rest ourselves in God's secret purpose behind nature's oddly perverse ways. But we do not forgive nature. Forgiving is only for persons.

Nor can we forgive systems. God knows that systems can hurt people. Economic systems can lock poor people in a ghetto of brutal poverty. Political systems can turn free people into slaves. Corporate systems can push people around like puppets and toss them out like trash. But we do not forgive systems. We only forgive people.

People are the only ones who can be held *accountable* for what they do. People are the only ones who can *accept* forgiveness and decide to come back to us.

Forgiving is always a personal event. It follows, then, that you should forgive *only* the persons who hurt *you*.

I do not need to forgive people who have not hurt me. In fact, I have no *right* to forgive them; only their victims have that right. I may be outraged at what they do to others. I may judge them, condemn them, and call for their heads to roll. I may, for instance, nurture a gargantuan rage at Joseph Stalin for his massive murder of Russian people. But, unless he injured me, I should not forgive him, not because he is too evil, but because he can be forgiven honestly only by the people whom he hurt. I would only cheapen the miracle of forgiveness if I claimed to forgive the great hurters of people who did not hurt me.

I do not mean that you have to feel the culprit's hands on your own throat. We often hurt most when we feel the pains of people we love. I, for instance, am almost neurotic about the way I feel the pain my children feel. If you hurt my children, you hurt me worse than if you assault me directly. In any case, we have somehow to *feel* the hurt ourselves or else we do not need the healing that forgiving was invented to give.

If forgiving heals the pains *we* feel, we have good reason to keep in touch with our own hurts.

Some of us deny the pain we really feel. It just hurts too much to acknowledge it. Sometimes it scares us; people betrayed and brutalized by their parents are often afraid to admit their pain for fear they may hate the people they most dearly want to love. So they use a thousand devices to deny their pain.

I sometimes deny my pain, not out of fear, but out of

23

sheer pride. I grit my teeth in heroic refusal to concede that certain people have enough power to hurt me. Just so, the betrayed wife says, "I know my husband has been playing around with that conniving little witch he calls his secretary, but I am not going to let him have the pleasure of seeing me suffer." So she shoves her pain into the dark room of the soul where feelings are not allowed to enter. And she may carry it off; she may outlast the secretary. But she will never forgive her husband as long as she refuses to admit to herself the pain she feels so deeply.

I am simplifying the scenario, of course. The story is not usually about an innocent lamb and a bad wolf. Most of us have to do our forgiving while we are being forgiven. And sometimes being forgiven gets so homogenized with forgiving that we can hardly feel the difference between them.

But in its essence, the miracle of healing happens when one *person* feels the pain and forgives the *person* who opened the wound.

UNFAIR PAIN

We always face a crisis of forgiving when somebody hurts us *unfairly*. Forgiving is love's remedy to be used when we are hurtfully *wronged* by a person we trusted to treat us right. There is a difference between suffering sheer pain and suffering painful wrongs.

It hurts to lose fifty dollars on a fair bet; it also hurts to be mugged on the street and robbed of fifty dollars. But there is a moral difference between what we lose fair and square and what we suffer in violent unfairness! It hurts a boy to be bawled out by his mother for slapping his sister; it also hurts when a child is screamed at by a drunken father for having been born. But what a difference between fair hurt and brutal wrong!

Not everybody is out to get us. Our lives are cluttered with people who wound our feelings in small ways, but who mean no real harm. We suffer some inevitable aches simply because we are vulnerable people living in a crazy world where fragile spirits sometimes accidentally collide.

For example: There was once a person in my life who did outrageous things to me. She screamed at me all through dinner; she made me jump to her service anytime, day and night, no matter how busy I was with other things; and now and then she would pee on my best slacks. To make matters worse, she got acutely sick and drove me mad because she did not tell me what was wrong. There were moments when I felt like whacking her. But I never felt an impulse to forgive her.

She was my six-month-old baby, and I did not feel a need to forgive the outrageous things she did to me, because she did not hurt me wrongfully. I loved her and I took whatever she dished out.

My example may be a little far-fetched, but it does make the point; we don't have to forgive people for every hurt we feel.

Many of us are hurt when we discover that an important human relationship we thought would last forever is, in fact, temporary. We part, we leave each other, and being left is often a very sour sorrow.

Some friendships need to be dissolved, some love affairs need to be ended. And leaving usually hurts somebody. But a wounded heart may be only the risk of love in a world where everything that comes must also go.

Perhaps the worst way for people to leave us un-fairly—yet without wronging us—is to get sick and die and leave us all alone. But people die because that is the way of nature; generally, they do not die because they want to hurt us. Still, how can a child understand that the father who got cancer and died did not really *mean* to leave her all alone? How sensitive we must be with people who know better with their heads, but who still *feel* wronged by someone who died and left them just when he was needed most.

It is harder still when those we love *decide* to die in spite of how much we needed them to stay alive. When Bob hung himself, he did not tell anybody what his motives were. Did he have to end his life? Is he to blame for the awesome pain he left behind? Should his wife forgive him? I cannot tell. Only she can know.

Sometimes you can't know for sure whether you have been the victim of an unavoidable accident or whether you have been wrongfully wounded. You may need help to sort out your hurts, so you can see the difference between feeling the pain that comes from our vulnerability and the pain that comes from being the butt of an unfair attack.

I do *not* mean that pain is unfair *only* when someone *means* to be unfair. Pain is unfair when we do not *deserve* it, or when it is not *necessary*. So you do not have to prove that someone *meant* to wrong you before you can forgive. You will be shoved into a crisis of forgiveness when you are needlessly knocked around, no matter what the other person's intentions were.

I have made a little catalogue of unfair hurts that everyone feels from time to time. In no case does the hurt-giver *mean* to be *unfair*. But in every case, we *experience* the hurt as an unfair assault. Match my list of hurts with your own experience.

PEOPLE HURT US BECAUSE THEY THINK WE DESERVE IT

Some people aim to hurt, they mean to do someone harm; but they want no more than just retribution. This is Shakespeare's Macbeth, resolved to do in his king: "I am settled, and bend up / Each corporal agent to this terrible feat." This is Booth taking aim at Lincoln in a theater. This is Lee Harvey Oswald plotting to shoot Kennedy on the streets of Dallas. This is Judas slouching into the night to betray his Master. Each one was doing what he felt his victim deserved.

I am pretty sure that almost everyone who has ever

hurt me on purpose sincerely believed I was getting what I had coming. A colleague of mine once wrote a private letter to my board to accuse me of some theological delinquencies. His letter was unfair to me, and it caused me a lot of trouble. I believe that my colleague meant to be fair. But what he meant and what I experienced were two different things. It *was* unfair, no matter if he *meant* it to be fair. And the unfairness of it threw me into a crisis: did I want to let it fester in my memory, or would I use the "magic eyes" and be healed?

Most people who mean to hurt other people believe they are being fair. They set out, teeth grinding, eyes steeled, lips tight, to do us harm in the belief that we deserve it. "It hurts me worse than it does you" is the ultimate piety of the person who intends to hurt but means to be fair. But what they *intend* does not take away the unfairness we *feel*.

When we are hurt in this way, we enter a crisis of forgiveness. We cannot relate to the person who hurt us as a friend or lover until we come to terms with the unfairness of the hurt.

PEOPLE HURT US COMPULSIVELY

Sometimes people hurt us, not because they want to do us harm, but only because they cannot control themselves.

Jack did not mean to hurt his family; he simply could not stay away from booze. Walter never intended to hurt his wife by having a sexual affair with another woman; he just could not harness his lively libido.

A year or so ago my friends Ben and Phyllis Sewall were slammed into as terrible a crisis of forgiveness as anyone has ever let me share. Their son, Roger, was idling his moped at a four-way stop on a lazy summer evening in Laguna Beach, California. Stopped, feet on the ground, he waited his turn to move on. A half-block behind him Sid Charid was gunning his Camaro down the same street in Roger's direction. He did not slow down for the stop sign. Roger, hit from behind, was killed almost instantly by a car he never saw coming. The driver stopped for a moment, then drove on, hit and run.

Sid, apparently, was high on drugs. He did not *mean* to hurt anyone; he was just out of control, driven by a mind-blowing chemical. But Roger did not deserve to die; nor did my friends deserve to lose their son. It was not fair. And this grotesque unfairness created as painful a crisis as any wounded heart can bear.

PEOPLE HURT US WITH THE SPILL-OVERS OF THEIR PROBLEMS

Sometimes our personal struggles, too turbulent to contain, spill over to affect innocent bystanders. We do not mean to hurt them; they just happen to be in the wrong place at the wrong time.

Children are sometimes the most unlucky victims of the pain that washes over from grown-up conflicts.

My friend Morgan was trapped in a miserable marriage and had good reason to want to escape. But his two little children happened to be living in the same house, drenched in the backwash of adult rage, sure that it must somehow be their fault that their parents hated each other. Morgan was only trying to get out of a hopelessly bad marriage. The last thing he wanted to do was injure his children, but they got caught in the crossfire. They did not have it coming; they were *wronged* as surely as they were hurt.

PEOPLE HURT US WITH THEIR GOOD INTENTIONS

Sometimes people hurt us even when they mean to do us good. Their well-meant plans go awry, maybe through other people's knavery, maybe by their own bungling. No matter how, what they do to help us turns out to hurt us.

The most generous friend I have ever had was Alec Morton, a selfless surgeon who gave two years out of every four to healing poor people in a shanty hospital on a mission compound in Burundi. He took no pay for

28

his work; he even brought along his own medications and gave them generously to the sick. He himself flirted chronically with borderline insolvency. But he cared a lot about his children and about their education. So he took the advice of a smart broker and sank all his savings into a real estate deal that, in a few years, promised to pay off well enough to see his six children through college and his wife through any troubles.

The payoff turned out to be a worthless piece of wilderness.

Alec's mind was on suffering people in Burundi and on security for his children. He intended it to turn out well, but his generosity was turned to unfair loss.

Alec—prone to depression anyway—sank deeper and deeper into the muck of self-condemnation. One night he drove up the hill behind his home and shot himself. His suicide was the unfairest cut of all. His children did not deserve to lose *him* as well as his money; and he was terribly unfair to them, no matter how good his intentions were. I think his children needed to forgive their father even if he was a saint.

PEOPLE HURT US BY THEIR MISTAKES

Sometimes we get hurt because other people make mistakes. They may be ministering professionals and they may surely mean to help, but sometimes they bungle the job.

Not many people can hurt us by mistakes the way doctors can. We trust them to take care of us; we let them put us to sleep while they slice our bodies apart and sew them together again. But they can err, and their errors cost us a lot.

When my mother-in-law was old and very sick she needed a massive blood transfusion. Somehow they managed to pump her veins full of the wrong type of blood. Nobody in the hospital meant to hurt her. Mistakes can happen to anybody. But she almost died. Unfairly!

A young intern, trying to impress his nurse, went

ahead on his own with a new treatment, when he should have checked first with the surgeon in charge. He prescribed drugs that, once inside of his patient, clashed with other drugs that she was taking; the medic should have checked more carefully, but he was in too much of a hurry, and the consequences were very painful and very unfair.

Mistakes, all of them! Everybody makes them sometimes. But when our doctors make them, we pay. We pay in extra hospital costs. We pay in pain that could have been avoided. Once in a while we may pay with our lives. And it isn't fair, no matter what the medics meant.

But enough! My catalogue of unfair hurts should be enough to remind you that the unfairness of the hurt often lies in the experience of the victim, not in the intention of the one who causes it.

Should you forgive someone who hurts you unfairly, but who never meant to do you wrong?

Not many people ever *mean* to be unfair. Even a Mafia hit man believes he kills only people who have it coming. So if we need to forgive people only when they *mean* to hurt us unfairly, we may never need to forgive anyone on earth.

In fact, you may *feel* the unfairness of your pain even more terribly just because the person hurt you carelessly. The drunk driver who kills your neighbor's child never meant to hurt anybody. But you may feel the horror of his unfairness all the more because of its pointlessness.

Perhaps more to the point, however, is our need to forgive *for our own sakes*. Every human soul has a right to be free from hate, and we claim our rightful inheritance when we forgive people who hurt us unfairly, even if their intentions were pure.

DEEP PAINS

The third dimension of the pain that needs forgiving has to do with depth. Hurts that need forgiving are deep hurts.

"Deep" is not a precise measure when it comes to pain; depth of pain lies in the hearts of people who feel the hurt. So we cannot be exact. We know for sure only when *we* feel the bruise. But surely we can at least agree on some rough differences between the superficial wounds that we can tolerate and the deeper hurts that separate us from the person who brought them on.

Here are a few of my own experiences of hurts that are really too shallow for a falling-out.

ANNOYANCES

Our lives are sprinkled with annoyances. I can't stand the kind of shoppers who check out fifteen items in the eight-item express lane and then talk about their cat with the cashier, while I wait impatiently to pay for one carton of milk. I drive my wife crazy by switching channels mindlessly on the television set. She annoys me when she stretches the short stories she tells at dinner into full-length novels. These are nettles against our tender skin; but they are probably not deep enough to raise the issue of forgiveness.

If we were to turn every nuisance into a crisis of forgiveness, our conversations would become revolving reconciliations. Better to swallow annoyances and leave forgiveness for the deeper hurts.

SLIGHTS

Slights are snubs, not as bad as being maligned, but bad enough to make us feel as if we've lost our standing in the pecking order. We want people to respect our place in the line-up, and we hurt whenever we lose our place.

Once, when I was a graduate student in Holland, I was invited to spend a Sunday evening at the home of a famous professor in Amsterdam. Monday morning, I bragged to my fellow American students and hinted that the great man and I had become close friends. A few weeks later, at a reception, I was standing with the same American friends when the renowned professor came into the room. We were all introduced to him. When he got to me, he did not remember ever having laid eyes on me before. He did not tell my friends that I was a worm, he did not spit at me or revile me. He just slighted me when I wanted badly to be noticed. I could have killed him. But I did not need to forgive.

Slights hurt because we are unsure of ourselves, needy creatures walking among people whose notice we need to support our self-esteem. We hurt when people walk by without looking at us; but we do not exile people from our lives for not noticing us. Slights are really for shrugging off, not for forgiving.

DISAPPOINTMENTS

We are hurt by people who do not do what we expect them to do for us. We invest our lives in our children; they take our investment for granted, as if they had it all coming. I was once a candidate for a cherished award; I did not get it, and I later discovered that my closest friend did not vote for me. A friend of mine stayed with his company out of loyalty when he was offered a better job somewhere else; when a position he wanted opened up his boss passed him by to promote a youngster waving a fresh M.B.A.

Disappointment! It can slap you in the face of your pride and leave you feeling cheated. Yet, though deeply disappointed, you are not betrayed and you don't need to forgive.

COMING IN SECOND

One mother gives her daughter all the advantages, more than she can afford; her daughter drops out of school and becomes a waitress while her best friend's daughter becomes an attorney. One student knocks himself out for a B while his roommate, who hardly tries, gets nothing but As. Your friend's horse prances into the winner's circle every race; your horse never manages to show.

When someone else gets the glittering prize you wanted, it smarts to come in second. The hurt is hardest to bear when the person who gets there ahead of you is a close friend. You have to put your arm around his shoulder and celebrate his good luck when you would really rather run away and drown your sorrows alone.

To be honest, we would feel better if our friends lost when we lost, their stocks tumbled when ours tumbled, and their kids failed when ours failed. But we do not quit a friendship because our friends got something we wanted, nor do we have to forgive them.

It is wise not to turn all hurts into crises of forgiving. If you need to forgive every minor bruise that you suffer in your run for a place in the sun, you will dam up the ebb and flow of all your fragile human relationships. We put everyone we love on guard when we turn personal misdemeanors into major felonies.

What sort of unfair hurt, then, does go deep enough to create a crisis of forgiveness? How do you know you have been hurt seriously enough to cause a falling-out? When does the wound require the radical spiritual surgery we call forgiving?

I will offer three examples of unfair hurts deep enough to bring us into a crisis of forgiving: *disloyalty, betrayal,* and *brutality.* Let me try to explain what I mean by each of them.

DISLOYALTY

I am disloyal when I belong to a person and I treat him or her like a stranger.

Most of us have several circles of people to whom we belong by personal bonds of loyalty. Inside the circle we are bonded to each other by a promise we have made to stay at each other's side. Sometimes the promise is made, head bowed, before witnesses, as a public vow. Sometimes the promise is tucked silently into what we do; a mother makes a silent commitment to care for her newborn baby simply by taking the child into her arms and two friends can vow a deep loyalty to each other without ever saying a word. Either way, our freely given promise to stay together and care for each other is the invisible fiber that holds us together; we belong to each other in the only way one human being may ever belong to another.

The promises we make *to* each other give birth to the trust we have in each other. People count on people who make promises. A baby counts on his mother to be there when he needs her. A wife counts on her husband to be there for her. A friend counts on a friend. Wherever people promise to be with us in care and support, we are bonded to them by our trust just as they are bonded to us by their commitment.

So when a father leaves his family in the lurch, he is disloyal because he has treated people who belong to him as if they were strangers. When a son makes a habit of lying to manipulate his parents, he treats them as strangers though he belongs to them by the bond of trust. A woman feels violated when she learns that her husband has played around with other women for several years because someone who belongs uniquely to her has treated her as if she were just another woman.

The loyalties of friendship may not be as binding as the loyalties of family, but if I discover that a friend let me down after he promised something to me—a favor, a loan, a blessing—let me down when I needed him badly, and only because he did not want to go out of his way for me, I feel as if the fundamental terms of our friendship had been violated. Someone I trusted to care for me as a loyal friend treated me as if he and I were strangers.

A person who breaks a promise of loyalty violates a relationship based on promise and trust. We cannot go on as usual in the relationship unless the wrong of it is healed. The hurt is too deep to go on as if nothing had come between us.

Disloyalty is not acceptable; it is offensive. We must either separate and carry the hurt alone or forgive the person who was disloyal to us.

BETRAYAL

Turn the screws a little tighter and disloyalty becomes a betrayal. My partner is disloyal to me when he treats me like a stranger, but he betrays me when he treats me like an enemy.

Peter was disloyal to Jesus when he denied that he ever knew the man. Judas betrayed Jesus when he sold him to his enemies for thirty pieces of silver. We betray people we belong to whenever we sell them out for a price.

Can anything hurt worse than a friend's betrayal?

We do not have to parlay for huge sums to be betrayers. Most betrayers are minor Iscariots, playing for petty stakes. A friend who tells another my special secret about my private shame, knowing that I may be hurt, betrays me. A husband who belittles his wife in front of guests commits minor treason. A close colleague who promises to support my bid for a promotion, but secretly signals to my boss that I am not competent to do the job, betrays me. A father who seduces his own daughter most certainly betrays her.

Caesar had his Brutus, his dearest friend who turned on him and slew him. But a friend, lover, spouse, or partner who lets others do us harm just as surely betrays us. No matter what the method is or how superficial the cut, we are betrayed.

Something lying close to our souls cannot indulge treason, not even trivial treason. We feel fouled and we feel diminished. Every human relationship built on trust is fractured by betrayal. To be friends or lovers after betrayal would be a sham. We know it is so because we feel the stab so deeply. And when we feel it, we are in the crisis of forgiveness.

BRUTALITY

As a rule, we forgive people who belong to us in

some way—spouses, children, parents, close friends. But sometimes we need to forgive strangers who bind themselves to us with a rope woven of brutality.

A stranger breaks into your home at night while you are asleep, vulnerable, alone in the ultimate privacy of your bedroom. You feel so personally violated that you cannot ever feel indifferent toward this man, not the casual way you feel indifferent toward an ordinary stranger who never got close to you. He did not touch you. You did not see his face. Yet, he came inside of your special private place where he had no right to be. He is not a mere stranger anymore; he is now, though faceless, a personal enemy.

Consider an assault far worse. A stranger rapes a woman in a dark parking lot. She is violated to her core. She does not know his name. She only felt his violence. But he can no longer be a mere stranger to her. He ravaged her and became her personal enemy; and because they are bound by violence, she is alienated by hate.

But brutal people are not always strangers. In fact, most brutal people assault those they belong to. Men who never sleep with other women beat their wives, and claim credit for fidelity. Fathers who would never desert their families batter their own children. We can be cruelest of all to people who belong to us.

There are also brutalities that never blacken an eye or break a bone. We can brutalize one another without touching. I have heard mothers tell their sons, for no good reason, that they were rotten kids, worse than worthless. I have known fathers who regularly told their daughters that they were no better than prostitutes.

At a party once, in Europe, I watched an American try to amuse his guests by coaxing his wife—who knew only Hungarian—to repeat English four-letter words that she would be horrified to speak had she known what they meant. I thought that he was brutalizing her as surely as if he had hit her. And I felt brutalized with her.

We are brutal whenever we reduce another person to less than human excellence. It may be a violent rape. It may be a degrading insult. Brutality, no matter who commits it, confronts us with one of the most agonizing crises of forgiveness.

So much, then, for the sorts of personal, unfair, and deep hurts that lead us into the first stage of forgiving.

Minor hurts that would ordinarily not call for forgiving can *become* major offenses by sheer repetition. For example, if Betty persists in an action just *because* it is annoying, and throws this petty annoyance at you regularly, she probably *wants* to demean you without having to risk too much. She wants to hurt you with her contempt, but she does not have the courage to make a frontal assault. Her annoyances then become moral injuries, and you cannot let her get away with it.

The same goes for slights. If your boss *always* forgets her appointments with you, her slight demeans you. If your father *never* takes time to listen to your troubles, his slight edges toward disloyalty. If your friend *never* calls you when he knows you are sick or in trouble, his slight slides into disloyalty because he treats you like a stranger.

How do you know when forgettable misdemeanors become insufferable felonies that need forgiveness? You can tell for sure only when you are on the scene. You cannot draw lines for others; you need to feel the difference for yourself. Some people turn all misdemeanors into felonies whenever *they* are hurt by them. Other people make themselves passive targets, inviting almost anybody to take a crack at them. But there is a difference, and one of the signs of growing up is the insight you need to tell the difference in the painful pinch of a moment when you are the victim.

CHAPTER 2

We Hate

Hate is a tiger snarling in the soul. Hate is our natural response to any deep and unfair pain. Hate is our instinctive backlash against anyone who wounds us wrongly.

But what is it that we feel when we feel hate for another human being? Especially when we hate someone we also love, or used to love?

Maybe we feel no more than a *passive* hatred—the grain of malice that robs us of energy to wish a person well.

I have felt passive hatred often—and, if the truth were known, so have other people who love at least as easily as I do. When I think about a man who once whispered lies about me, I cannot find it in my heart to hope that he will be a great success in his work. I do not wish he would die; I simply have no desire for him to do well while he lives. At the very least, I don't want him to do better than I do. I cannot raise an honest prayer that he will become a bright star in the little sky we share.

On the other hand, there is an *aggressive* fury that drives us out of our wits. A woman wishes her former husband would catch herpes, or at least be miserably unhappy with his new wife. You hope the friend who hurt you when he told your secret will get fired from the new job he found. We may settle for lesser retribution, or we may wish our enemy would drop dead. In any case, we are not only drained of the positive energy to wish someone well, we devoutly wish them ill. We are poised to attack. This is *aggressive* hate.

When you hate passively, you lose love's passion to bless. When you hate aggressively, you are driven by a passion to whip someone with a hurricane—or at least a stiff March wind—of hostility.

Passive or aggressive, our hate separates us from those we ought to belong to. It shoves them away from us. Where? Any place where no good can reach them or harm can miss them. Hate is the elemental inner violence that drives people apart.

Sometimes hate divides our own souls; one part of us hates and the other part loves. And we both hate and love the same person. A wife loves her husband for his sexy attractiveness and hates him for his savage put-downs. A husband may love his wife's devotion to their marriage and hate her for her pallid indifference to his needs. We love the father whose love we gasp for; we hate him for driving us crazy with a love he keeps just beyond our grasp, like a prize held just out of reach. Oh yes, we could play the love-hate duet infinitely.

The point is that hate's searing flame coexists with love's soothing flow; the hate that pushes us apart lives inside us right along with the love that pulls us together. Indeed, we can hate most painfully the people we love most passionately.

Hate eventually needs healing. Passive or aggressive, hate is a malignancy; it is dangerous—deadly, if allowed to run its course. Nothing good comes from a hate that has a person in its sights; and it surely hurts the hater more than it hurts the hated.

We must not confuse hate with anger. It is hate and not anger that needs healing.

Anger is a sign that we are alive and well. Hate is a sign that we are sick and need to be healed.

Healthy anger drives us to do something to change what makes us angry; anger can energize us to make things better. Hate does not want to change things for the better; it wants to make things worse. Hate wants

39

to belch the foul breath of death over a life that love alone creates.

Let me point out some things about hate that make it such a hard sickness to cure.

IT IS PEOPLE, NOT MERELY EVIL, THAT WE HATE

It is said that we are supposed to "hate the sin and love the sinner." If we manage to do this, our hate can be creative. But I must admit that I do not easily find the power to do this—the evil I hate wants to stick to the person I hate the way skin sticks to the body, and I can seldom tear them apart.

So I am not talking about hating cruelty; I am talking about hating cruel *people*. I am not talking about hating treachery; I am talking about hating *traitors*.

If David betrays me, and I hate him for hurting me, it is because my mind cannot separate his action from his person. He and his broken promise are one reality, stuck together within my hurting soul.

This is the pain, this person-directed hate; it is not health, it is not strength, it is the soul's sickness.

None of us wants to admit that we hate someone. It makes us feel mean and malicious. So we deny our hatred. We hide it from ourselves. Hate is too ugly for us; we cannot admit that we have a bucket full or even a spoonful of it in our system. We deny, we disguise, and we suppress the real hate that ferments in our souls.

But we do hate people. Only an unearthly saint or an unfeeling oaf gets far in life without hating someone, sometime—passively, at least, and now and then with the bursting belligerence of aggressive malice.

When we deny our hate we detour around the crisis of forgiveness. We suppress our spite, make adjustments, and make believe we are too good to be hateful. But the truth is that we do not dare to risk admitting the hate we feel because we do not dare to risk forgiving the person we hate.

We make believe we are at peace while the furies rage within, beneath the surface. There, hidden and suppressed, our hate opens the subterranean faucets of venom that will eventually infect all our relationships in ways we cannot predict. Hate left to itself, denied and hidden, leaves us in a cold hell behind insulated masks of warm conviviality. Hate, admitted and felt, compels us to make a decision about the healing miracle of forgiving.

Why worry about it? Why fret so much that decent people hate people who do them wrong?

The reason is that hate focused on people is very hard to heal. When we only hate the wrongness of a thing, our hate dies when the wrong we hate is righted. But when we hate people who do us wrong, our hate stays alive long after the wrong they did is dead and gone, the way the ashen smell of charred lumber lingers with a burned building long after the fire is out.

We attach our feelings to the moment when we were hurt, endowing it with immortality. And we let it assault us every time it comes to mind. It travels with us, sleeps with us, hovers over us while we make love, and broods over us while we die. Our hate does not even have the decency to die when those we hate die—for it is a parasite sucking *our* blood, not theirs.

There is only one remedy for it.

WE MOST OFTEN AIM OUR HATRED AT PEOPLE WHO LIVE WITHIN THE CIRCLE OF OUR COMMITTED LOVE

We usually hate someone who is close to us—close enough to love. We hate the person we trusted to be on our side, the person we expected to be loyal, the person we trusted to keep a promise.

We do not usually hate strangers. We get angry at strangers. At baseball games I have raged at the cross-eyed umpire and gotten mad at the loud drunk sitting near me. But I have never hated an umpire I didn't know personally, or a drunk I never saw again. The only time we really hate strangers is when they get close enough to violate us intimately.

Hate for people within our circle of committed love is the most virulent kind. It does not affect us so much when we hate a person who never promised to be with us, never walked with us on our private paths, never played the strings of our soul. But when a person destroys what our commitment and our intimacy created, something precious is destroyed. Hate for people we love makes us sick.

The virus resists every antibody save one.

WE HATE PEOPLE WE BLAME

Whenever I hate someone I pronounce that person guilty of hurt in the first degree, and I hold that person responsible for hurting me personally—I blame them. I refuse to excuse Howard's brutality on the grounds of his own brutal childhood. I cannot suspend judgment on Jean's unfaithfulness on grounds that she is only a hapless victim of torrid hormones. If they have hurt me, I feel hatred for them.

Unless we are a little crazy, we hate only the people we blame for doing us wrong.

Our hatred is a compliment, in a strange sort of way. The hated person is set apart from other creatures and honored as a free person. Our hate tells us that this person has a will and he used this will to do us harm.

When we hate a person who deserves our hate we feel very righteous in our hating. The jerk has it coming. What we feel is precisely what we ought to feel. Heaven and earth would shake if we did not hate the person who meant to do us harm.

Holy hatred is the toughest kind of all to cure. Only one remedy is worth prescribing. But it comes hard. And the longer we hate, the harder it is to heal us.

I recall Michael Christopher's play *The Black Angel*, where he tells the story of Herman Engel. Engel, a German general in World War II, was sentenced by the Nuremberg Court to thirty years in prison for atrocities committed by his army. He survived his sentence and was released from prison. At the time of the play he is in Alsace, building a cabin in the woods where he and his wife intend to live out the years left to them— incognito, forgotten, at peace.

But a man named Morrieaux, a French journalist, is waiting in the wings.

Morrieaux's whole family had been massacred by Engel's army during the war. When the Nuremberg court had refused to sentence Engel to death thirty years before, Morrieaux privately condemned Engel to die. His condemnation was kept alive and hot by the fire of hate he kept kindling in his heart. Now the time had come.

Morrieaux had stoked up the fanatics in the village close by Engel's cabin. That very night, they were going to come up the hill, burn down the cabin, and shoot Engel and his wife dead.

Morrieaux, however, wanted to get to Engel beforehand. Some gaps in Engel's history plagued the reporter's need for a finished story. So he went up the hill, introduced himself to a shaken Engel, and spent the afternoon grilling the former general about the village massacre that lay like a forgotten shadow in Engel's past.

But Engel's feeble humanity—he seemed less like a monster than just a tired old man—confused Morrieaux. Besides, he was having a hard time putting all the pieces of the terrible story together; and so he was plagued by newborn doubt. His vengeance was blurred; the purity of his hate was contaminated.

Toward the end of the afternoon, as the sun fell deep and the woods became a cavern, Morrieaux blurted out to Engel that the villagers were going to come and kill him that night. He offered to lead Engel out of the woods and save his life.

But the afternoon's inquisition had brought other kinds of doubts into Engel's soul. Engel paused, eyes fixed on a cone just fallen from a black pine: "I'll go with you," he slowly said, "on one condition." What? Is he mad? Does he lay down a condition for having his own life saved? What condition?

"That you forgive me."

Forgive? Morrieaux had exterminated Engel a thousand exquisite ways in the fantasies of hate that he had played in his mind for thirty years. But face to face with the ambiguity of Engel's humanity, Morrieaux's vengeance was unsettled. He would save the man's life. Yes, he would cancel the execution.

But forgive him? Never.

That night, the enraged villagers came with sacks over their heads, burned the cabin, and shot Engel and his wife dead.

Now I ask, why was it that Morrieaux could not forgive Engel? Why was forgiving even harder than saving Engel's life?

It was too much for Morrieaux, I think, because his hatred had become a passion too long lodged in his soul. Morrieaux could not live, could no longer be the person he was without his hatred; he had *become* his hatred. His hate did not belong to him, he belonged to his hate. He would not know who he was if he did not hate Engel.

The tragedy was that only forgiveness, the one thing he could not give to Engel, could have set Morrieaux free.

Hate can be fatal when we let it grow to enormous size inside of us. The best of people can get their bellies full of it. And it is just as real whether it involves a nasty little scene between friends or a question of international immorality.

Sometimes hate only nibbles at the edges of the heart; it does not always burn out the lining of the soul. Sometimes it only asks that the hated person keep away from us for a while; it does not always go for the jugular.

But whether your hate is a carcinoma growing hell-bent for death inside your soul, or only a pesty heartburn, it will hurt you if you do not use the right remedy. Your healing may take heroic surgery of the soul. Then again, you may get by with a quick cauterization. But eventually, unchecked hate will do you in.

Such hate *can* be healed, however, and it is to the healing that I invite you next.

CHAPTER 3

We Heal Ourselves

We are ready to take our first step inside the healing heart. Pull your mind away from the person who needs to be forgiven; do not ask yet what happens to the forgiven wrongdoer. Look only at the wounded forgiver. Think only of Fouke and his "magic eyes." Never mind Hilda for the time being.

When you forgive someone for hurting you, you perform spiritual surgery inside your soul; you cut away the wrong that was done to you so that you can see your "enemy" through the magic eyes that can heal your soul. Detach that person from the hurt and let it go, the way a child opens his hands and lets a trapped butterfly go free.

Then invite that person back into your mind, fresh, as if a piece of history between you had been rewritten, its grip on your memory broken. Reverse the seemingly irreversible flow of pain within you.

The first gift we get is a new *insight*.

As we forgive people, we gradually come to see the deeper truth about them, a truth our hate blinds us to, a truth we can see only when we separate them from what they did to us. When we heal our memories we are not playing games, we are not making believe. We see the truth again. For the truth about those who hurt us is that they are weak, needy, and fallible human beings. They were people before they hurt us and they are people after they hurt us. They were needy and

45

weak before they hurt us and they were weak and needy after they hurt us. They needed our help, our support, our comfort before they did us wrong; and they need it still. They are not *only* people who hurt us; this is not the deepest truth about them. Our hate wants to cloak them, top to bottom, only in the rags of their rotten deed. But the magic eyes of forgiving look beneath the tattered rags and let us see the truth.

New insight brings *new feeling*.

When forgiving lets us see the truth about our enemies, it gives us a new feeling toward them.

When we talk of feeling, the word "irrelevance" may help. When you forgive me, for example, the wrong I did to you becomes irrelevant to how you feel about me now. It does not matter, does not count, has no bearing, cannot be figured into your attitude toward me, the person you hated until now. The pain I once caused you has no connection with how you feel toward me now.

Of course, we cannot pry the wrongdoer loose from the wrong; we can only release the person within our *memory* of the wrong. If we can peel the wrong away within our forgiver's memory, we can see the person who really lives beneath the cloak of the wrongdoing.

Forgiving, then, is a new vision and a new feeling that is given to the person who forgives.

The Bible talks the same way when it describes how God forgives. In the ancient drama of atonement, God took a bundle of human sins off a man's back and tied it to a goat. He gave the goat a kick in the rear and sent it off, sin and all—a scapegoat—to a "solitary land," leaving the sinner free of his burden. Or, as the poet of the Psalms put it, he wipes our sin away, as a mother washes grime from a child's dirty face; he removes it from us as the East is removed from the West, and "ne'er the twain shall meet."

A scapegoat? A washed face? It is poetic language for what God does *within his own mind*. He changes his memory; what we once *did* is irrelevant to how he *feels* about what we *are*.

It is like that when *we* first forgive someone. When you forgive your friend Linda, you may be the only person healed. You do not have power to woo Linda back into your life. She is out of your control. It could be that she does not give a fig for your forgiveness; maybe she would prefer your hate, maybe your hate for her justifies her hate for you. So when you forgive you must often be content with the editing of your own memory. It is the editing of your memory that is your salvation.

If you cannot free people from their wrongs and see them as the needy people they are, you enslave yourself to your own painful past, and by fastening yourself to the past, you let your hate become your future. You can reverse your future only by releasing other people from their pasts.

Forgiving is an *honest* release even though it is done invisibly, within the forgiver's heart. It is honest because it happens along with honest judgment, honest pain, and honest hate. True forgivers do not pretend they don't suffer. They do not pretend the wrong does not matter much. Magic eyes are open eyes.

How can you tell when it happens?

If the first stage of healing is release, and if release happens in your vision of the person who hurt you, is there an early sign that your healing has begun? Is there a clear symptom of the onset of forgiveness?

You will know that forgiveness has begun *when you recall those who hurt you and feel the power to wish them well*.

Forgiveness is love's antidote for hate, beginning with passive hate, the loss of energy to wish people well. So, when we feel the slightest urge to wish that life would go well for them, we have begun to forgive; we have started to release those who hurt us from the blight of the harm they did to us.

This sign of the healing stage of forgiving was made clear to me as I talked with my friend Myra Broger about forgiving her former husband.

Myra is a beautiful woman, an actress, who was

47

almost killed by a hit-and-run driver a few years ago. She was left crippled, but still gorgeous and luminous. Her husband, a TV and film star, stayed with her only until she recovered from the accident. Then, coldly and quickly, he took off and left her alone.

I asked Myra if she had been able to forgive him. She said she thought so. I asked her what made her think so. "I find myself wishing him well," she said. I bore down. "Suppose you learned today that he had married a sexy young starlet, could you pray that **he** would be happy with her?" I expected her to bristle at my pushy insensitivity. But she responded almost casually, "Yes, I could and I would. Steve needs love very much, and I want him to have it."

I was skeptical. She sounded far too simple and sweet. But I came to know that her forgiveness was genuine, and that she was living within the free flow of a healed memory. She really did wish him well!

A modest beginning, to be sure. Not yet an Olympic plunge into a new relationship. I do not know whether her magic eyes make any difference in the life of her former husband, but they make all the difference in the world to Myra's life. The hate is gone; and when the mortar of hate goes, the wall eventually crumbles.

The act of forgiving, at this stage, has not achieved its climax. It is not yet the embrace of two people simultaneously released from the grip of a painful past.

Many profound thinkers do not want the healing of the memory—short of climax—to count as forgiveness. Take the late American theologian Paul Tillich, for instance; he says that "genuine forgiveness is participation, reunion overcoming the power of estrangement." In Tillich's opinion forgiving does not really happen unless people are brought together in a renewed relationship—close, intimate, mutually accepting. Forgiveness completed, fulfilled in the coming together of two people, is the only genuine article.

I think Tillich was wrong; I think we can have reality even if we do not have the whole of it. We can have a great experience climbing a mountain even if we never reach the peak.

Sex can be good—if not all we want—even if orgasm escapes us; forgiving can be real even though the person we forgive is out of our reach. We need not deny ourselves the healing of incomplete forgiving; we can forgive and be free in our own memories.

But forgiving does create a momentum that, left unbraked, can carry a healed person back to the one who wounded him.

Let us move on to the next stage, then, the new beginning, the place where we who are separated come together again.

CHAPTER 4

We Come Together

I have always liked the way Scottish theologian H. R. MacIntosh talked about forgiveness. Forgiveness, he said, "is an active process of the mind and temper of a wronged person, by means of which he abolishes a moral hindrance to fellowship with the wrongdoer, and reestablishes the freedom and happiness of friendship."

Abolishing the "moral hindrance to fellowship"—this is the key to complete forgiving.

Remember that it is what people *do* to us that creates the "hindrance" to our getting together, really together, in spirit as well as in space. When people hurt us unfairly and deeply, the *wrong* they do comes between us. They make us feel wronged in a way we cannot easily brush aside. And we know in our heart of hearts that things will never be right between us if we ignore the *wrong* that separates us.

If we ignore the "moral hindrance" as if it did not really matter, we take our first step into an opiated life where nobody really gives a damn.

It is not a matter of our being too touchy; we are not overloading on peevishness and pique. We are only holding on to respect for what we are and for what has to be right between us if the two of us are going to have honest love between us.

Only the magic eyes can take away the "moral hindrance" in the heart and mind of the forgiver.

Now let's say that your magic eyes have done their healing work in your mind and heart. You have emptied out your hate and doused your lust for getting even. You no longer need the sour satisfaction of revenge.

But what will it take to *"reestablish the freedom and happiness of friendship"*?

Both parties—the wronged and the wrongdoers—must bring about an honest coming together. Magic eyes cannot do this part alone.

You hold out your hand to those who did you wrong, and you say: "Come on back to me, I want to be your friend again."

But when they take your hand and cross over the invisible wall that their wrong and your hate built between you, they need to carry something with them as the price of their ticket to your second journey together.

If they cannot or will not pay their fare, you will have to settle for your own healing, your private freedom from hate, your own inner peace.

What must they bring?

They must bring truthfulness. Without truthfulness, your reunion is humbug, your coming together is false. With truthfulness, you can make an honest new beginning.

But what is truthfulness?

Truthfulness is a state of mind; it has to do with your real intentions. You must want your words to carry your real intentions. What you say must vibrate with what you feel in your heart. Harmony between the message you give to the outside world and the feelings you keep on the inside.

But there is one thing more about truthfulness, just one thing. You must at least try to bring both your heart and your words in tune with reality.

This is the truthfulness those you forgive must bring with them as their entrée back into your life.

To be specific, you must expect those who hurt you

to be honestly in touch with the reality of your falling-out, your pain, and their responsibility for them.

FOR ONE THING, THEY MUST TRULY UNDERSTAND THE REALITY OF WHAT THEY DID TO HURT YOU

They need to *know* that the pain you suffered at their hands was unfair to you. You did not deserve to feel the hurt; no matter what was meant by it, you suffered what you should not have had to suffer.

They also need to know that the hurt they caused you went *deep*. Deep enough for you to feel that you could not go on as before unless something happened to remove it. They may be dumbfounded that their little lance could have sliced so close to your heart. Never mind. People are always surprised at how much their "little" faults can hurt other people. The point is that you felt it so deeply that you could not let them come near you and share what was left of your heart in the same way it was shared before. And they must, with their mind, feelings, and words, reflect the truth of your hurt.

You cannot expect them to agree with you about every little detail. No two people in the history of personal misunderstandings have ever remembered their painful experience in the same colors and the same sequences, because no two people have experienced the same hurt in precisely the same way. So, if you want total recall, blow for blow, insult for insult, hurt for hurt, you will never get what you need.

But they must be truthful about what happened in the eye of the storm of your sad falling-out. And you need to believe that they are truthful before you can let them all the way back into your life.

THEY MUST BE TRUTHFUL WITH THE FEELINGS YOU HAVE FELT

To be truthful with your feelings, they must *feel* the hurt that you feel. What they know intellectually must percolate to the bottom of their heart. It is not enough to admit that they hurt you; they must feel the very hurt they hurt you with. Their feelings need to be one with your feelings.

How can they feel your pain? They can feel your pain as it echoes deep within them. You felt their disloyalty as an unfair cut that made you hate them enough to turn them into partial strangers. Now they must feel as if their *real* selves are strangers to the persons they were when they hurt you; they must hate themselves for what they did to you.

Their pain and your pain create the point and counterpoint for the rhythm of reconciliation. When the beat of their pain is a response to the beat of yours, they have become truthful in their feelings. Their feelings are moving to the tempo of your feelings. They have moved a step closer to a truthful reunion.

THEY MUST BE TRUTHFUL IN LISTENING TO YOU

They cannot give you truthfulness in their words alone. The truthfulness of a soliloquy is never enough to reunite two people. So, in your coming together, their honesty must be born in listening. The price of their ticket into your life is an open ear; an open mouth gets them only half way.

They must listen to you until they *hear* your claims and your complaints and your cries. At first they will filter your message through the screen of their own desires and fears. They will want to reshape every little syllable you speak until it suits the message they want to hear you speak. So you must make sure they have listened long enough.

And you must also listen to their response, to make sure that they really did hear you. You must lure them into a response, several times over, seduce them into many repetitions, until you can be sure that they are truly hearing you, and hearing your needs as you reveal them. This is the only way you can know they are being truthful.

THEY OUGHT TO BE TRUTHFUL ABOUT YOUR
FUTURE TOGETHER

For two people who are coming together again after a falling-out, truthfulness requires a promise made and a promise meant to be kept. Those who hurt you must return to you with a promise that they will not hurt you again; and you need to believe that they intend to keep the promise they make.

They promise to be there for you in the future, when you need them, to be there in a style that lives up to the kind of relationship you have together.

You should not ask for a lot more; but you should ask for no less. They cannot offer you a guarantee; they cannot be depended on the way you might rely on a computer or a well-trained dog. They are ordinary, fallible human beings; they are not God. You lay a bet on them; you need to take a risk. But if they are truthful, they *intend* to keep their promise. And their honest intentions tilt the odds in their favor.

You don't have to have total truthfulness before you can *begin* to forgive them. The forgiving you do to heal the wounds in your memory has no strings attached; it is your free act of grace, done for yourself within the innermost cells of your soul. The demand of truthfulness is for the *fulfillment* and *climax* of your forgiving, the coming together again of two people who once belonged to each other and were separated from each other in their spirits.

We have been speaking of the requirements for reconciliation. Now we can shift our focus and talk about the *realistic limits* of every coming together.

We come together within the unrelenting boundaries of our time and of our circumstances.

Time shapes all our reunions with a mastery that not even the miracle of free forgiveness can loosen. We cannot turn our calendars back to a happier day. Time does not let us come together as if nothing had happened between our falling-out and our forgiving. We change personally, and we take on new roles; we cannot simply abandon our new places in life the moment a friend is forgiven and invited back into our lives.

If you have forgiven another person and want that person back in your life, you must be realistic enough to ask this question: What has happened to each of us between our falling-out and our forgiving?

Sometimes, I know, the time has been mercifully brief and our roles unchanged. A woman forgives her husband for his blundering infidelity. He wants terribly to come home to her; he has languished in the loneliness of his true love's unsatisfied needs. She opens her arms. Chances are he will sail back to her on the frenzied winds of recharged eros. Their coming together may be a sexual crescendo, ecstatic, enough to make them both playfully grateful for the separation that rekindled their stormy hankering after each other.

Not always so. Maybe she has forgiven her husband a hundred times for putting her down in the presence of handsome young women. She forgives him and takes him back again, not with a voluptuous bedding down, but with a muted sigh that whispers nothing more seductive than, "Well, let's get on with it then." But they do get on, and they bind their lives together with the invisible thread of loyalty, strong enough at least for a new beginning. Not a rapturous embrace; but better, no doubt, when all is said and done, than staying strangers separated by hate.

Sometimes, given the way things have stacked up since the falling-out, you have to do with a very limited sort of reconciliation. My friend's husband wronged her so badly that she found no way to go on with him. They had a spiteful divorce, and afterward she hated him lavishly for leaving her out in the cold while he found warm love nestled in the lap of a woman twenty years younger. But that was four years ago, and she has since forgiven him; she released him as she let her hate go away, and as she was able to see him for the needy person he really was. So she invited him back into her life. But he could not come far.

He has been married for three years, to the woman

he loved too much while he was still married to my friend. So their coming together will have to leave them at a distance. He can be a friendly *former* husband, and she will wish him well with the woman she hated him so much for loving. Maybe they will talk on the telephone and trade stories about the kids; maybe the children will get them together for an hour on Christmas Eve.

We cannot breathe back all the old life; we forgive and reunite on the terms that time and circumstance make available to us.

I know a splendid woman who is struggling to forgive her father and wants some sort of reconciliation with him. Her father is a fundamentalist preacher who knows right from wrong in every nook and cranny of everyone else's life. He proclaims the judgment of an angry Almighty for every infraction of any of his rules; his ways are very narrow and his gates very straight. Nonetheless, he sexually abused my friend when she was a little girl, convincing her that a father who lived close to God could do no wrong. She left home at seventeen to get away from him and swore she never wanted to be near him again.

Now, after fifteen years of alienation, she is freed from her hate, and wants him to be her father again. But she knows she cannot take him back into her life as a little girl welcomes her daddy home. She cannot be a child to him again.

Their roles will be reversed; she may have to take care of him and let him be a child to her. In any case, she cannot have her deepest wish—to crawl back into his lap, resting in his strong arms, finding the loving care he once betrayed by twisting love into cruel abuse. If it is possible for them to come together again at all, she knows it will have to be a reunion that cannot give back her lost childhood.

Here is a sad little story that is heard more and more these days. Jack and Jan were more than good friends once, but Jack was married and Jan was not. The

56

sexual part of their friendship eventually destroyed the rest of their friendship altogether. Jack made promises he could not keep and then cut the knot quickly, crudely, cruelly, leaving Jan very empty. She filled the void with hate. She was badly wounded, and for two years raged against Jack for using her. Then ever so gradually, and to her own surprise, she forgave him. She was healed.

But she could not bring Jack back to their true love of three years before. Their reunion, honest as it is, must be long-distance—letters, a Christmas card, a conversation on a busy corner, concern for each other's well being, no more. Reunion within the bounds of reality.

We practice love's high art framed and fringed by the boundaries of time and place. We heal the wounds of our painful pasts, but the healing is limited by things that have happened to us during the time since our falling-out began. We make our new beginnings, not where we used to be or where we wish we could be, but only where we are and with what we have at hand.

Accepting limits is its own kind of honesty. Wine out of water, OK—but, please, not out of Elmer's glue! New beginnings must fit within the arena of one's own circumstances. The only day we ever have to forgive each other in is *this* one, the day we have at hand; and with the options we have on this particular day we must make our new starts on the adventure of reconciliation.

We start over, too, in the semidarkness of partial understanding. We will probably never understand why we were hurt. But forgiving is not *having* to understand. Understanding may come later, in fragments, an insight here and a glimpse there, *after* forgiving. But we are asking too much if we want to understand everything at the beginning.

You must start over again in your mysteries. He is a mystery to you. And you want to be a mystery to him.

There is a lot more to you than meets his eyes, he must know that. So you can share each other's private demons and secret angels, and leave yourselves room for wonder at one another. As long as you are ready to move on with him without first unraveling his mystery, your shared mysteries can unfold as you go.

CHAPTER 5

Some Nice Things Forgiving Is Not

When you forgive the person who hurt you deeply and unfairly, you perform a miracle that has no equal. Nothing else is the same. Forgiving has its own feel and its own color and its own climax, different from any other creative act in the repertoire of human relationships.

Forgiving gets its unique beauty from the healing it brings to the saddest of all the pains. We need to do it at all only because we live in a world in which human love can be fractured by unfair suffering. It has something in common, in this respect, with the beauty of artful surgery. But precisely for this reason, as the healing of wounds left open from our painful pasts, we should not let it slip into a sloppy blend of several other nice things people can do for each other in unpleasant situations. We need to develop a fine taste for the distinctive quality of the forgiving art.

So let us go on from here and test our sense for the subtle difference between the miracle of forgiving and other things we need to do in order to get along well together in our unfair world.

FORGIVING IS NOT FORGETTING

When we forgive someone, we do not forget the hurtful act, as if forgetting came along with the forgiveness package, the way strings come with a violin.

Begin with basics. If you forget, you will not forgive at all. You can never forgive people for things you have forgotten about. You need to forgive precisely because you have not forgotten what someone did; your memory keeps the pain alive long after the actual hurt has stopped. Remembering is your storage of pain. It is *why* you need to be healed in the first place.

Forgetting, in fact, may be a dangerous way to escape the inner surgery of the heart that we call forgiving. There are two kinds of pain that we forget. We forget hurts too trivial to bother about. We forget pains too horrible for our memory to manage.

We don't remember every trivial hurt, thank God, not *all* the bruises we have felt from people along the way; if it doesn't go deep, we let it heal itself and we forget. An old friend came to me not long ago to ask me to forgive him for something he did to me that I could not remember, not even when he tried to stir my recollection. He needed to be forgiven, he said. I persuaded him that I felt for his needs, and that I would be his friend just as if he had never told me, but that I could not forgive him. If he had brought back old pain by bringing back my memory, I should have forgiven him. But as it was I could not really forgive him; I could only love him and by loving him heal the separation that he felt, though I did not.

The pains we *dare* not remember are the most dangerous pains of all. We fear to face some horrible thing that once hurt us, and we stuff it into the black holes of our unconsciousness where we suppose it cannot hurt us. But it only comes back disguised; it is like a demon wearing an angel's face. It lays low for a while only to slug us later, on the sly.

Forgetting can be Russian roulette, the same sort of game a woman plays when she "forgets" the little lump she felt on her breast a month ago.

Enough, then, to light up a warning sign: never mistake forgetting for forgiving.

Once we *have* forgiven, however, we get a new

freedom to forget. This time forgetting is a sign of health; it is not a trick to avoid spiritual surgery. We *can* forget *because* we have been healed.

But even if it is *easier* to forget after we forgive, we should not make forgetting a *test* of our forgiving. The test of forgiving lies with healing the lingering pain of the past, not with forgetting that the past ever happened.

True, the Bible says that God promises to forgive us *and* forget. Jeremiah speaks for God: "I will forgive their sins, and will remember their sins no more." But does he forget the way we forget when we can't remember where we left our keys? Of course not. God does not have amnesia; to say that God forgets is to say that he *feels* about us the way he *would* feel if he *had* forgotten.

We are the same. Can you stop your memory on a dime, put it in reverse, and spin it in another direction the way you can reverse direction on a tape recorder? We cannot forget on command. So we just have to let the forgetting happen as it will; we shouldn't rush it, and we certainly should not doubt the genuineness of our forgiving if we happen to remember.

The really important thing is that we have the power to forgive what we still do remember.

I will say more about forgetting later on, and about a healing way to remember bad things. But enough for now: forgiving and forgetting are not the same.

EXCUSING IS NOT FORGIVING

Excusing is just the opposite of forgiving. We excuse people when we understand that they were not to blame. Maybe the devil made them do it. Maybe there were extenuating circumstances. They were not to blame. So why should we forgive them? We forgive people for things we blame them for.

We excuse people because we understand why they

had to do what they did. A French proverb says, "To understand all is to forgive all." But this is not quite right. We only *excuse* all if we understand all.

It takes no saving grace to excuse someone. All excusing takes is a little insight.

We all need a lot of excusing. All of us are what we are partly because of what other people have made of us—our parents, our teachers, our ancestors.

We were dealt a hand of cards when we were born, and we have had to play our game with those cards. Some of our cards were strong; we were blessed. But there were some jokers in the hand as well. Surely we do not need to be forgiven for the weak cards that were in the hand that was dealt to us, cards we did not ask for and have never wanted. All we can be blamed— and forgiven—for is how we played the hand we were dealt.

Think of the reasons you could submit to show someone that you were not to blame for the rotten thing you did.

Your genetics. An X got where a Y was supposed to be in your chromosomic building blocks; your genetic structure is shaky. The fault lies in your DNA. You do not need forgiving; you need to be re-engineered!

Your psychic conditioning. You had a crazy up-bringing; your father was passive-aggressive and your mother was manic-depressive. Together, they made you what you are today. You do not need forgiving, what you need is therapy.

Your culture. Your culture made you what you are. You were conditioned to do whatever in your culture gave you pleasure and to avoid whatever in your culture caused you pain. We do not have to forgive you for anything; if we want to help, we can change the culture that made you.

You see, there is no grace needed. All it takes is a little savvy about how human beings work.

But when you finally say, "There is no explaining what they did," we have, at that moment, admitted the mystery of their free choice and we have come to where the crisis of forgiving lies.

Sometimes, frankly, the difference is a matter of very delicate shading. Frank Kooster and Leo Sedman come floating out of my boyhood to show how subtle the difference between excusing and forgiving can sometimes be.

First, Frank. One summer in Michigan I was picking cherries from one of those tall, rickety stepladders that get you high enough to reach the top branches of a cherry tree. A few trees away, I could hear Frank Kooster saying terrible things about me to a stranger. He couldn't see me, but I heard it all; and I felt as though I had died.

Frank had become my special friend. Every summer, when I was ten or so, my mother took me to visit some old friends of hers, people she had known back in the old country, who lived on a farm about fifteen miles up a gravel road from our house in Muskegon, Michigan. Three days on that farm were our summer's vacation. They were my idyll, the more so as I got to the age when farm boys did men's work.

When it actually came to doing the jobs, though, I was badly miscast, badly enough to make a farmer thank the Almighty he had no son with my lack of aptitude. I really did fail farming.

But Frank, a real farmer's farm boy, embraced me and took me in. I felt like an insider with Frank; we had sat on the ample seat of a tractor for hours in the fields, had walked on the same path as we flanked the cows coming in for milking, had pitched new mown hay side by side. I felt we were bonded by our hours of silence in the sun, by the secrets of the soil we shared, the nest of baby rabbits we almost plowed under but skirted around instead because Frank had an eye for the slightest variation in the ground's make-up, the bucket of baloney sandwiches we ate together for lunch in the shadow of a MacIntosh apple tree at ten in the morning. Oh yes, we were bonded all right.

That day in the orchard he was picking cherries too, with a farmer friend his own age, a few trees from where I was picking, hidden from view, but not out of earshot.

He was gossiping about his parents' friends from the city—us. I heard it all. Pete and Wes, my brothers, were fine, good guys. But Lewis is good for nothing, he said. "He wouldn't know enough to come in out of the rain if it was hailing coconuts. He's worthless."

Me? Yes, Frank was bad-mouthing *me*. The one person, above all others in the world, I wanted to like me was telling a stranger that I was a bust, a fizzle, a wash-out, a piece of wasted creation. I felt stabbed.

Yet, as I remember the moment now, I find myself excusing Frank for making me feel outcast. He was only sizing up reality as he saw it, through the only lenses he had available to him—the lenses of a farmer. He was not interested in the possibility that I might survive as a traveling salesman, or a jazz singer, or maybe a preacher. He judged me as a farmer, the way a baseball scout sizes up the potential of a bush-league third baseman. Who cares if the guy can do calculus if he can't hit a curve ball?

So, Frank is excused; he is almost blameless in my eyes.

Leo Sedman is different; he needs to be forgiven. Leo was the coach of the Muskegon High School football team, the Big Reds, when I was a skinny kid trying to run through the obstacle course of what they smirkingly called physical education.

What did they care if a kid was ashamed to show his skinniness in the locker room? I hated my body. I hated the bony bumps where other kids were smooth and round. More than anything else, I hated the hip bones, the pointed nubs that jutted from my sides like swords sticking out from twin scabbards beneath the flesh.

The moment of painful truth came to me at the end of every gym period, when the curtain went up on my side-bones. Shower time! Twice each week, my side-bones were flung on center stage in the boys' locker room! Every kid in the class would look at the bones and—I knew it in my heart—would laugh inside and be glad he was not made like me.

So I cheated. I would get undressed, open my locker door, fiddle with it, and wrap a towel around the hip bones. I would shuffle, cagey, over toward the showers, hang around just outside them for a minute or two, whistling, eyes on the locker room door, just in case the coach walked through, with the towel casually draped over the bones. Then I would amble back over to my locker, unshowered, and sneak my clothes back on over my sweaty body.

Mostly I got away with it.

One day big Leo caught me; he waddled right up to my locker, the very head coach of the Big Reds, standing right alongside me. Leo was big, really big; hipbones cushioned under three layers of the most beautiful fat a toothpick kid could covet. He must have weighed 300 pounds. And there he was, looking me over, hard-eyed, tight-lipped, tough. He had been watching me, he bawled. Well I had better believe him, buddy boy, that I was not going to get away with it. He would teach me not to cheat on the shower. Off with my clothes, and into the shower, while everybody gawked.

A crowd of kids came around, like a bunch of people at a curb where a man lies bleeding. They were all looking at me, grinning, waiting for me to bleed and die. Good show.

Leo knew what he was doing. He was out to hurt a kid who was ashamed of his body. He was a college graduate, trained in the human behavior of skinny kids, six feet tall. Somebody could put up a case for him, I suppose; maybe a fat man needs to be reassured that fat is nicer than skinny. But I think he knew what he was doing. And I cannot excuse him.

You were guilty, Leo Sedman, and I hated you. Boy, did I hate you. All I can do with you is forgive you.

Forgiving is tough. Excusing is easy. What a mistake it is to confuse forgiving with being mushy, soft, gutless, and oh, so understanding. Before we forgive, we stiffen our spine and we hold a person accountable. And only then, in tough-minded judgment, can we do the outrageously impossible thing: we can forgive.

FORGIVING IS NOT THE SAME AS SMOTHERING CONFLICT

Some people hinder the hard work of forgiving by smothering confrontation. When they are in charge of the shop, they never let people heal conflict through forgiving; they stage-manage conflict so that people never get a chance to forgive.

Some parents are dedicated to smothering conflict. They shush us and soothe us and assure us that whatever makes us mad is not worth raising a fuss about. They get between us and the rotten kid who did us wrong, always protecting, always pinning down the arms of our rage, forever pacifying. Their "now thens" and "there, theres" keep us from ever unloading our anger and from ever forgiving. They say, "Forgive and forget," but what they mean is: "Don't make a fuss, I can't stand the noise."

Ministers tend to be compulsive managers of conflict. The church needs controversy no more than Arkansas needs a tornado. So if the vestryman's wife is involved in hanky-panky with the organist, and somebody threatens to blow the lid, smother it, keep it out of sight until we can get the mess swept under the rug of churchy discretion. If a deacon is put down by the chairman of the board and wants to thrash it out at the next meeting, smother it, get the deacon to see that nobody will like him if he raises a hullabaloo. We must have no confrontation.

There is a lot to be said for managing conflict. Goodness knows not many of us are good at it. My meager message here is only that we should not confuse the technique of smoothing things over with the high art of forgiving those who transgress against us. Quieting troubled waters is not the same as rescuing drowning people, and smothering conflict is not the same as helping people to forgive each other.

ACCEPTING PEOPLE IS NOT FORGIVING THEM

We accept each other *because* we *are* acceptable *in spite of* blemishes that sometimes make it hard. People come to us with a cluster of unacceptable qualities; but we accept them as our friends anyway. We spot fine people slouching behind a brush of disagreeable traits. So we accept them *because* of what they are, or can be, to us—in spite of what we have to get through to find them.

Accepting a person can feel a lot like forgiving. But it is not the same.

The difference between accepting and forgiving is very simple. We accept people *because of the good people they are for us*. We forgive people *for the bad things they did to us*. We accept people for the good they *are,* and we forgive them for the bad they *did*.

It will help us see the difference if we look at three ways we have of accepting people. First, *social* acceptance. Second, *professional* acceptance. And, third and most difficult, *personal* acceptance.

We accept people *socially* when we embrace them inside of our community. Some of their customs may be odd and distasteful to us. Their lifestyle may stick in our craw. We may not take to their ways at all. But we accept them, not necessarily as people we want as friends, but as people whom we reckon deserve a place of respect within our group.

We accept them socially because they qualify socially. We have no call to forgive them for anything; they have not hurt us unfairly. We just accept them within our group even though there may be things about them that we do not much like personally.

We accept people *professionally* because we need to accept them in order to help them. The really nifty people-accepters are our friendly therapists. We can spill all our beans to them without having to worry that they will throw us out. "Hmm, you would like to shoot your mother-in-law through the head. Interesting. Oh, you want to sleep with your sister-in-law? Yes, of course, I understand. No, no, I don't think it is terrible for you to want to sleep with her. Do you?"

Our broad-spirited counselors ignore all our oddities, overlook our weird inclinations, and treat us with unconditional regard. They make us feel accepted, unjudged, secure.

But what is happening is *not* forgiveness.

For one thing, we did not hurt *them*. They would need to forgive us if we were trying to seduce their spouse, or if, God forbid, we refused to pay their bill. But, in their *professional* relationship with us, they accept us "in spite of" our neuroses, and they do not confuse this acceptance with forgiving. So much for the technique of accepting people for professional reasons.

We accept people *personally* as our friends or our lovers because they are worth a lot to us in spite of a lot of things about them we would rather do without.

A wife accepts her husband in spite of his odd need to tell dirty jokes in company once he has had a drink or two. And he has to accept her compulsion to hover over him like a mother hen to see that he does not drink too much, or eat too much, or pick his nose in public.

No marriage could last, no friendship survive, no family endure if we could not see each other as people worth accepting beneath our crazy-quilt patterns of kinks and cranks. We accept the people we love partly because we are committed to them, no doubt, but also because, on balance, tolerating their quirky habits is a decent trade-off for the good things they bring to our lives.

When we forgive a person we do more than overlook a blemish for the sake of the beauty behind it. A woman who forgives a lover for betraying her secret knows that when she forgives him she does something very different from what she does when she accepts him in spite of his bad breath.

There is one right word for the amazing moment when we release a person who dug a deep hurt into our lives. The right word for this moment is not acceptance. The right word is forgiveness.

FORGIVING IS NOT TOLERANCE

Forgive me and you heal yourself. Tolerate everything I do and you are in for a lot of trouble.

You can forgive someone almost anything. But you cannot tolerate everything.

Whenever people try to live or work together, they have to decide on the sorts of things they will put up with. The group that puts up with everything eventually kills itself.

Take my friend Joe, a squatty, balding Italian who sold bargain bread out of a tired old store in a nervous neighborhood on the border of blight. We used to buy bread from Joe at half the supermarket price, and kids came from a mile around to buy sweet rolls from him with a good chance of getting a sugar-sprinkled doughnut thrown in. Joe turned second-day bread into a symbol of a neighborhood trying hard for a second time around.

One afternoon, near closing time, three neighborhood kids walked into Joe's store, pulled a gun, cleaned out the cash, and then, for no reason, one of them—a kid named Sam—shot Joe in the stomach. He almost died.

While Joe was in the hospital, the parents of the kid who shot him came to see him. They were decent, devout folks, poor like most people in the neighborhood, and now bent heavy with shame. One night they brought Sam; nobody ever thought they could get him to come.

Joe forgave Sam. He decided he was going to look at Sam as a weak human being who needed a chance instead of as the rotten kid who shot him in his stomach. In fact, he talked with Sam's parents about giving him a chance to earn a little money cleaning out the store.

But Joe never meant to put up with shooting people in the stomach. Nor was his neighborhood ready to tolerate what Sam did.

So when Sam came to trial, Joe was a sad but convincing witness for the prosecution.

Sam spent a year at a juvenile detention center.

Take Pastor Gambit, a man with an enormous appetite for human adoration, especially female, preferably up close, and prone if at all possible. He cultivated quite a knack for parlaying spiritual counseling into erotic campaigns, and before long he had more than a few adoring women singing ecstatic doxologies in response to his secret ministrations. So many, in fact, that he could not keep them all quiet about it. The upshot: Gambit became the center of scandal.

He was charged with ministerial malfeasance in the court of the church.

Some of Gambit's colleagues (who knew that there, but for the grace of God, went they) made a pitch for the court to forgive him, in the style of Jesus, who once turned to a woman guilty of a like sin and said to her: "Neither do I judge you, go and sin no more."

But the kindly clergy were getting forgiving mixed up with tolerance. Gambit needed forgiveness all right, from somebody. But the court's job was not to decide whether Gambit could be forgiven, but whether the church could tolerate what Gambit had done.

Take a different sort of situation, one where no one offends morality, but where a bad judgment threatens efficient procedure.

Dr. Harry Den Best runs an elite surgical team at Atlantic Medical Center where he is head heart surgeon and where the brightest and best young surgeons on the East Coast get their start toward the brilliant career they assume is their birthright. But the limits of tolerance for goofs in Den Best's operating room are so narrow that few students make it through residency at Atlantic without a chronic case of terror.

Some mistakes are tolerable—*once*. Anybody using a tough technique for the first time can fumble. Even a second time, though, they had better come up with a good excuse. A third time? Better start thinking of a residency in Sioux Falls. But there is one error that Den Best does not tolerate even once: an intern or resident surgeon does not initiate a new medical procedure for a Den Best patient without consulting him first.

Dr. Fred Bush, a brilliant but arrogant young resident, was in the unit one night when one of Den Best's patients in intensive care took a turn for the worse about twelve hours out of surgery. Something had to be done, but it was 2 A.M. and Bush knew Den Best had to be in the operating room again at five. Why wake him up? So Bush wheeled the patient back into the O.R., where he, on his own, patched her up brilliantly.

Ten minutes after Den Best arrived at Atlantic that morning, Dr. Bush's career, like Den Best's patient, took a quick turn for the worse. The best hope Bush has now is a secure residency at a general hospital in central Iowa.

Den Best could have personally forgiven Bush; but he could not tolerate what Bush had done. Bush had gone beyond the tolerable even though he was well within the range of the forgivable.

Every group has to decide what it will put up with and what it cannot tolerate. But what we need to remember is this: we don't have to tolerate what people *do* just because we forgive them for doing it.

71

Forgiving heals us personally. To tolerate everything only hurts us all in the long run.

Let me put together the sum and substance of what I have been saying in this chapter.

You do not *have* to forget after you forgive; you may, but your forgiving can be sincere even if you remember.

You do not excuse people by forgiving them; you forgive them at all only because you hold them to account and refuse to excuse them.

You do not forgive people by smothering conflict; if you forever smother people's differences, you rob them of a chance to forgive.

You do not forgive people merely by accepting them; you forgive people who have *done* something to you that is unacceptable.

You do not have to tolerate what people do when you forgive them for doing it; you may forgive people, but still refuse to tolerate what they have done.

Part 2

FORGIVING PEOPLE WHO ARE
HARD TO FORGIVE

A wonderful woman recently told me how, long ago, some men she never saw and whose names she never knew had done a thing so terrible to her that it changed her life forever. Her story helped me to see how hard some people are to forgive.

She was a dark Armenian beauty, with black eyes that bore into mine as if she were trying to seduce from my eyes what my words were not giving her: release from her painful memory of the worst thing any human being could do to another. How could I give her a key to freedom from the hate that possessed her for almost a half century, glowing like incense on the altar of holy vengeance?

Whom did this splendid lady need to forgive? She needed to forgive men with no faces and no names, a gang who invaded her home one late night in Teheran and slaughtered everyone in her family. She had grown up in Iran, early in the century, moderately upper class. One night five terrorist Turks with hoods over their heads came to her house and tied up her husband and her two children, her father and her mother, dragged them out of the house and outside the city and butchered them all. She lived only because, unlike most any other night, she was away on an errand for the prep school where she taught Iranian children.

"Tell me," she softly demanded, "tell me how I can forgive people who have no faces, no names, no numbers, but were real enough to murder my children?" I felt an awesome turbulence moving inside her gentle confrontation.

Her problem was the faceless anonymity of those who did evil against her. Can you forgive the invisible people, the ones whose faces you cannot see, but who do you terrible wrong?

I have told you about my gentle interrogator so that she could lead us into what we must talk about next: people who are very hard to forgive.

It is hard to forgive people we cannot see, or touch, or maybe even know.

It is also hard to forgive people who do not care whether we forgive them or not.

It is hard to forgive some people because they seem too evil to be forgiven.

And it may be hardest of all to forgive ourselves.

But what about God? Some of us have wondered, in tough times, why God let us down when he could have helped us? Can we forgive God? Do we dare ask?

I invite you to explore with me the lives of some of these people, the kind that are very hard for us to forgive even when we want both to forgive and forget.

CHAPTER 6

Forgiving the Invisible People

Some people invade our lives for a tragic hour or a sad lifetime, leave us with hurting memories, and then move away where we cannot see them. They are invisible, people whose reality is now woven from the thin fabric of a time that no longer is. They are not less real to us than people we see before us, people with faces and names and bodies to touch. They are only harder to reach with our hands and with our forgiveness.

People become invisible when they die before we can forgive them. Or when they hide their faces behind the masks of corporations. People become partially invisible, too, when they do not leave a clear picture of themselves in the minds of their victims—mentally handicapped people, and children, hurt by people whose faces they can only dimly see.

Walk with me slowly through a few fields of the most fragile feelings that can haunt a human memory.

THE PARENT WHO DIED

I know a woman who hates her father for inflicting her life with a bad memory of the perverted sex games he made her play with him when she was too young to say no to Daddy. Now he is dead.

She hates him. But she hates herself even more.

She is sure she cannot free herself from the hatred

she feels for herself until she forgives her father. But how does she forgive a father who is not here to say, "I'm sorry"?

Most of our mothers and fathers were ordinary people with ordinary flaws. They do not need to have been savage slatterns or raging bulls to make them hard to forgive. Morally straight parents who could not love their children may be as hard to forgive as morally bent parents who molest their children. But once they become invisible, they are all terribly hard for us to forgive.

No matter, then, whether we were walloped by a hot-tempered father or hung out to dry by a cold-hearted mother—why is it so hard to forgive parents who pulled a fast one on us by dying before we got the freedom to forgive them?

Dead parents are hard to forgive for the simple reason that they are so far out of reach. We cannot hug them after we forgive them. We can't crawl on their laps and let them love us now the way we needed it then; and they cannot tell us how sorry they are. They cannot do any of the reconciling things that make forgiving a little easier.

Dead parents are hard to forgive, too, because something in us does not want our departed parents to need forgiving. We want to remember a saintly mother and a noble father, and to forgive them means to catalogue them with ordinary folk. It isn't nice to hate someone—and then to forgive someone—who sacrificed so much to get us to make something of ourselves. Especially if they have died and gone to heaven.

Still, hard as it is, a lot of us need to forgive dead parents if only for the sake of peace within our own living selves. And we can do it.

Keep in mind these facts when you try to forgive your dead parent.

NO PARENT IS PERFECT

No parent is a god, few mothers are saints, and

hardly any fathers deserve to be idols. Even "ideal parents" are at best gentle folk, and gentle people do cruel things. You will not shake the foundations of life if you admit that your father could have been cruel to you and your mother could have left you in the cold.

Once they are dead, we want our parents to be sheer light, with no darkness in them at all; and we feel a little foul if we allow shadows to darken our memory. We don't want them to *need* forgiving; because if we forgive them, we must have found fault with them first, maybe even hated them. I still shudder when I think about forgiving my mother. She gave her body and soul to put food in our stomachs and steer us toward godliness and a steady job. You could go to hell, I thought, for hating a mother like her. Yet, she had a shadow side, as every parent does. And I learned that hate does not have to cancel love, that I could love her as much as I ever did, and still hate and forgive one part of her.

If you feel a need to forgive a dead parent, you must face up to the reality that your father or mother could truly have done you wrong.

OUR PAINFUL FEELINGS ARE VALID

You may remember childhood hurts, and one part of you may hate the parent you blame for them; but you do not dare to *feel* the pain and do not dare to *feel* the hate. We do not dare let ourselves follow our feelings into their depths because we are afraid the pain will be unbearable and the hate too ugly for us to admit.

There is a flow to feeling that can, if you follow it, carry you to its own deep well. It will carry you to the depths if you are willing to put away your defenses.

If you let them, your feelings can take you into terrible nights of awesome sadness. You will feel again the loneliness of your childhood struggle to be loved. You will feel again the dread of not being good enough for a parent's love. You may feel as if you are lost, without hope and without light, such feelings as you would hardly dare admit to your best friends.

And they can take you into an ugly place where you will feel the heat of your hate. Even hatred for a saintly mother or a beloved father! They may lead you into your own private hell. But there is no freedom to forgive your dead parents unless you let yourself *feel* the pain you need to forgive them for.

Your feelings, of course, may be exaggerated. They may also be distorted. No matter. They are *what you feel*. So they are valid. And you find freedom to forgive your dead parents when you admit the validity of your feelings about them and when you let yourself *feel* the pain you want to forgive them for.

YOU NEVER COMPLETELY FORGIVE A DEAD PARENT

You can't finish the four stages of forgiving when you forgive a dead parent. Perfect forgiving ends in a reunion of two people estranged by hurt and hate. But when death intervenes, this happy ending is postponed for a time beyond all earthly relationships. You must be satisfied for now with a healing of memory.

You may not even complete your *own* healing; the cure may need to be repeated many times. Forgiving dead parents works a lot like quitting smoking; you may need to start over again several times before you finally pull it off.

YOU NEED TO FORGIVE YOURSELF EVEN AS YOU FORGIVE YOUR DEAD PARENTS

The hurt we get from parents almost always makes us feel guilty or ashamed of ourselves; I have never met a person who hated his father or mother who did not also hate himself.

Most people who try to forgive their dead parents have a frightened hunch that they deserve the miserable feelings their parents left them with. Ask a woman who was sexually molested by her father what the worst effect of it is. She will probably tell you that the worst part of it is the way it made her hate her own self.

Even if our parents were saints, they could get us to hate ourselves by infecting us with the hatred they felt for themselves. My own saintly mother developed self-accusation into a fine art. The fact is that she had little time and less energy to do much hard-core sinning. Yet she remembered every little sin she did manage to sneak into her life, and she ruminated over it and inflated it until she felt like one of the great sinners of the age.

To us she was both holy and heroic; but her goodness only made things worse for us. If a saintly mother could not forgive herself, how could moral midgets like us ever forgive ourselves?

I discovered after she died that I could forgive the mother who nurtured my self-hatred only when I forgave the self I hated. But I honestly do not know which came first, forgiving her or forgiving me.

But dead parents are not the only invisible people.

THE INVISIBLE MOTHER WHO GAVE HER CHILD AWAY

Here is a conversation we have heard at our house more than once:

"Why should I?"

"Because I asked you to."

"Why should I do what you ask me to do?"

"Because I am your mother."

"You are not my mother."

"I am your mother and I love you."

"You *never were* my mother and I *hate* you."

The angry young lady in the conversation was our daughter Cathy, a flaming hothead of sixteen at the time, a beautiful lady of twenty-six now, and our best friend. The woman she was raving at was my wife, Doris.

As we look back on those rip-roaring domestic tempests and as we enjoy our friendship now, we are sure that the toughest challenge for adopted children is their struggle to forgive the invisible birth-mother who gave them away.

When Cathy was a little girl we put the best possible face on it for her: "She gave you away because she loved you too much to keep you." Maybe so. But somewhere in her heart, Cathy wondered whether it wasn't just the other way around; maybe her birth-mother gave her away because she was not worth keeping. Besides, if she loved her *that* much, Cathy suspected, she could have kept her if she had really *wanted* to; what she probably wanted was to get rid of a baby who could only get in the way of what she really wanted out of her own life.

In any case, Cathy had to hate somebody. She had every right. Being given away and adopted can be a crummy way to be smuggled into a family nest. And since the invisible birth-mother who gave her away was not around to hate, why not hate the visible parents who were all too close at hand? *Our* love was only a reminder to her that somebody else had let her go. So she carried a double load of hate.

The only remedy for the pain of her hate was her power to forgive.

But how do you forgive a mother who has no face, no name, no address? How *does* an adopted child forgive an invisible mother?

I will share my sense of how Cathy came to be healed by the power of forgiving. I do not mean to suggest that every adopted child has to move toward forgiveness along Cathy's route. But it can't be *wholly* unique to her.

One thing Cathy did was to get *some* information about her biological parents. Not everything. She did not track them down and meet them face to face, as some adopted children do. But she learned enough about them to get a feel for their personal reality: they were very young, they were poor, they belonged to religions that did not seem to mix, and, of course, they were not married. *And* she learned that her birth-mother was Italian, a delightful "explanation" for the romantic spirit in Cathy that her sober Dutch parents could never tame. Her birth-mother became a more *real* person to her, even though she was still invisible.

Then Cathy learned more, and in a new way, about the agonies a young woman goes through before she decides to give her baby for adoption. One of her special friends became pregnant and, after upheavals of fear and doubt, gave her child to a childless couple for adoption; Cathy loved her friend deeply, shared her terrible conflict, and was sure that, all things considered, her friend did the right thing for her child. She came to feel in a new way how her own birth-mother was probably a wonderful person who was caught in a terrible conflict and really did give her away because she loved her too much to keep her. Cathy was too smart to believe that it was *all* love and no self-interest; but she came to see that there could have been *enough* love to make it true that she was given away because she was loved too much to be kept. Her new empathy with her natural mother did not wash out all of Cathy's hatred, but it did bring it down to forgiving size.

Cathy's next move was the most important one of all. She came—with help—to see herself as she really was, a splendid, strong, intelligent, and valuable person. Having been given away as a baby could not diminish her own superb worth as a woman. But here too, she was smart enough to see herself as a mixed bag. She needed forgiveness as much as she desired to be applauded.

Finally, she came to believe that God forgave her invisible mother, for whatever wrong she did. And if *God* could forgive her birth-mother, why shouldn't *she* forgive her too? And, for that matter, why shouldn't she forgive herself in the bargain?

I do not want to give the impression that Cathy walked an easy and straight line to freedom and peace. But she did it; she managed one of the toughest jobs in the whole arena of forgiving: she forgave the invisible person who brought her into the world and then gave her to us.

Doris and I have muddled through the rearing of three adopted children. They have handled the forgiving challenge in their own ways. Not one of them has done it the same way as the others. But each has proven to me that forgiving is the only remedy for the hurt of being given away as a child.

THE INVISIBLE GHOST BEHIND THE ORGANIZATION

People sometimes hide behind organizations and hurt us with institutional systems.

Their faces are hidden from us by desks and boardroom doors, secretaries' smiles, and minutes of committee meetings.

They are the invisible people we need to forgive when the organization hurts us and we hate the organization for doing it.

For Bob it was the textile factory where he worked in Boston for twenty-five years, without a day's work lost for sickness; the company "released" him without a pension when it moved to cheaper labor in South Carolina.

Charlie was promoted to a job that gradually got too big for him to do. He had put in twenty years, the best years he had to give. But they fired him at an age when no other company was likely to pick him up. And they hired two people to replace him at the job they had asked him to do alone.

For some, it is something much worse.

Organizations have little grace. They can knock you down, drag you across a bed of nails, throw your remains into the street, and, just before you hit the pavement, hand you a ten-dollar plaque with your name on it to show the company's gratitude. Organizations are amoral; they can leave you bleeding in the street with no breathing human being around to accept the blame: it is all company policy.

So you end up hating an impersonal organization.

What do you do when you hate the organization and your hate is tarnishing your golden years, turning you into a crotchety, maybe surly, but surely wounded old soul?

What you have to do is find yourself a living, breathing, responsible *person* in the organization and forgive that person (or persons, if more than one were involved).

If you were thrown out of your job before your time by a callous company policy, you must not try to forgive the impersonal company. You will never pull it off. You need to find a vice-president or a personnel manager, someone who could have seen to it that you were treated fairly. And, if you can, you should make an appointment for a confrontation. He or she will probably put you off with a reasonable explanation. But it is better to forgive someone whose name you know and who may not be solely to blame than to be saddled for the rest of your life with the pain caused by an impersonal system.

You shouldn't waste your soul's vitality trying to forgive an organization. The secret to peace is: get to a person behind the corporate facade.

Chances are he or she will tell you the system was to blame. You mustn't let the company's spokesman off the corporate hook too quickly. You must declare him or her guilty of second-degree hurt, at least, and then you can use the power that God gives you to hold your hand out to the vice-president or the foreman and say, "I forgive you." After that, you are on the way to healing. Only *on the way*. But it is enough for starters.

PEOPLE BADLY OUT OF FOCUS

Some people cannot get a clear picture of the culprits who did them harm because the "cameras" in their brains are out of focus. But they, too, need to forgive those who wrong them.

I wonder how mentally retarded children forgive people whose identity is always fuzzy in their eyes. Is a Down's Syndrome child equipped with special powers to forgive?

When I wonder how intelligent a person has to be to forgive someone, I always think about Toontje. I am not proud to tell it, but I want to tell it so that I can show how easy it is to hurt somebody who cannot get a firm fix on the person doing the hurting.

In our graduate student days, I was living with Doris on the grounds of a large mental hospital outside a village called Bennebroek, in Holland, where we had splendid rooms in a rambling Dutch mansion. The grounds of the hospital were landscaped like a park, with winding walks lined by oaks and dotted with patches of hyacinths, tulips, and daffodils. The beauty of the place encouraged me to take a snappy walk every morning through the hospital grounds and alongside the flowered fields.

It was on my walks that I met Toontje, close to noon every morning. Toontje ("Little Tony" in English) was microcephalic; his brain was too small to organize his world or learn the alphabet.

But Toontje learned to perform one useful service. He had a smallish cart with two large buggy wheels for easy steering, a straight handle for pushing, and two legs behind the wheels so the cart could stand almost upright when Toontje parked it. He also carried a stick about three feet long, with a sharp point on one end for stabbing pieces of paper along the sidewalks of the hospital grounds.

You could see him every morning jabbing at crumpled cigaret packages or chewing gum wrappers, carrying them to his cart, pulling them off his stick, and cautiously laying them there, one by one.

If he walked a ways without finding any litter to pick up, he would provide his own. He would stop his cart, lift out a piece of paper, carry it to the edge of the sidewalk, drop it to the ground, walk back to the cart for his spear, stalk the piece of paper, pierce it through, carry it back, and soberly deposit it back into his barrow. Toontje was exercising his human right to be useful.

How, you may ask, did Toontje know when it was time to call it a morning and head back to Building Nine for his lunch? Simple. He had learned to ask one question and to recognize the one answer that gave him his signal. He learned to ask: *"Hoe laat is't?"* ("What time is it?"). When he heard one answer— *"Twaalf Uur"*—he knew it was time to turn the cart about and head home. So, with his respectful, squeaky drawl, he asked everybody he passed on the hospital walks: *"Hoe laat is't?"* Everybody, every morning— same question.

One sunny Dutch morning I spotted Toontje poking his studded stick through another crumpled cigaret pack, and I felt a nasty impulse of the sort that leads decent persons to do very mean things.

What would Toontje do if I asked *him* his own question?

My timing had to be exquisite. I had to catch Toontje on the very verge, lips puckered for the H in *Hoe,* and then sneak in my question before he had a chance to ask his.

"Hoe laat is't, Toontje?"

He froze. His hand dropped limp from the handle of his cart, his eyes gaped, fixed on blank space, and he began to shake, first his hands, then his head, and his entire body quaking, while from his mouth came inchoate stuttering sounds. He shook for all of fifteen horrible seconds and then he gradually put his hands back on the handle of his cart and pushed it past me, not looking, not saying anything.

I knew the evil I had done the moment I saw him shake. In the conceit of my temptation I thought it was a harmless game, maybe even a psychological experiment. But after I did it, I knew what it really was that I had done: I had demeaned a person who had no tools to play my unfunny game with me. I had betrayed my brotherhood with this man, and hurt a child of God who did not have it coming.

Could he forgive me? Were my chances of forgiveness less with Toontje than with a nasty Ph.D.? Could this man with a brain too small to count change get a clear enough focus on me and what I did to him, even to sense that I needed forgiving? Or is it possible that a large heart made up for his small brain?

I do not know whether Toontje, and all other people who are short-changed on cerebral skills, are given a special power to forgive. Toontje died some time ago. In heaven, I'm sure, Toontje learned what a wretched thing I had done to him that April morning twenty years before. He also got a clear profile of me as the person who did it. And I am sure he forgave me, though I never deserved it.

When we meet maybe he will teach me how people with small brains forgive people with small souls.

I think we are all like Toontje in our own ways. Everyone is at bottom a mystery to me, just as I was a mystery to Toontje. I can never get a perfectly clear fix on anyone. The difference between the partial way we all understand each other and the partial way Toontje understood me is really not all that great.

We all see and know each other in part, as through a glass darkly.

So we forgive in part, too.

CHAPTER 7

Forgiving People Who Do Not Care

The scenario of forgiving does not always end in a happy reunion. Sometimes the story is suspended in mid-air, where the response to our forgiveness is, "I couldn't care less."

A person who hurts us and does not care digs the first wound deeper and makes the miracle of forgiving ever so much harder.

We do not want to forgive someone who laughs at our pain. For that matter, we do not rush to forgive someone who just shuffles off and leaves us alone to suture the cuts he sliced into our life.

When someone hurts us meanly, we want him to suffer too. We expect this clod to pay his dues; we want him to grovel a little. The old-fashioned word for what we want is *repentance*.

But the people who hurt us do not always come through.

The question is: should we forgive them anyway? Does it even make sense to forgive someone who would rather we keep our forgiveness and feed it to the dog?

Before we decide, we should make sure of what we want. What do we want people to do for us when we ask them to repent?

Not every hurt calls for repentance, any more than every cut needs stitching. In the cross-town traffic of human relationships we have limitless chances to rub people the wrong way, thoughtlessly, carelessly, and stupidly. But we do not dig a ravine between each other every time we get hurt. Mini-wrongs can be soothed with a modest gesture that falls well short of repentance.

An *apology!*

Apology? What a conversion that word has had! In the old days, an apology meant a plea of innocence against a dreadful charge. Today we apologize when we plead guilty to a trifle.

The other night my wife came home in a stew about a crude male who shoved his way into her place at the gas station. It was raining, hard. Doris was fourth in line at the self-service lane, where there was one diesel pump that could be gotten at from either side. Three cars were lined up ahead of her. When it was finally her turn at the pump, she got out of the car, put her back to the pump while she spun off the gas cap, and then turned to reach for the nozzle. But a new station wagon full of family splashed up in the other lane; the driver sprang out of the front seat, grabbed the nozzle just as Doris reached for it, and then took the cap off his own tank and whistled while he filled it with diesel fuel.

My wife watched him, buffaloed, and then pulled herself together to make her counterattack. "You saw that I had been waiting in line for this pump before you got here." "That makes no difference to me," he said. "I think what you are doing is contemptible." "I don't give a damn what you think." "Your children are watching; do you care what they think?" "Look, lady, I told you I don't care what *you* think."

She recycled the dialogue to me as if I stood for every rude macho driver in the world: "He would never have dared to do that to me if I had been a man!" Probably not.

Would an apology do? Suppose she met the man next week at the same pump and he offered to let her move ahead of him and said, "Sorry about last week, the kids had been driving me mad, I was in a dreadful hurry to get home, and I was terribly late." I think

Doris would have gulped and grudgingly indulged him. His apology would have done the job.

Apologies keep life oiled when the bearings begin to wear. Nicely timed and sincerely meant, the graceful apology is a curtsy to civility, a gesture that helps crowded citizens put up with each other with a smidgin of courtly humor, a modest bow to keep the hassle within tolerable bounds.

All the more reason, then, to see that apologies do not try to do the job that only repentance can do.

Powerful and sneaky people use apologies as end runs around repentance. They betray a trust; and, when they have been found out, they say they are sorry for "mistakes in judgment." They smile through their oily apologies when their crime calls for quakes of repentance. They get by only because we have lost our sense of the difference between repentance for wrong and apologies for bungling.

Ordinary people do it too. We do something painfully wrong, but when we are called to account we try to slide through our fault on a slippery apology: "Oh, my dear, you *are* exaggerating. But if you insist, I'll say I am sorry, so let's forget it." A quick maneuver around the pain of penitence!

We should not let each other get away with it. A deep and unfair hurt is not a mere *faux pas*.

We cannot put up with everything from everyone; some things are intolerable. When somebody hurts us deeply and unfairly an apology will not do the job; it only trivializes a wrong that should not be trifled with.

If Jackie apologizes for having betrayed you, you must call her bluff and throw her "Sorry about that" into the garbage disposal. If Fred lies about you after he promised to be your friend, you must accept no apologies from him; you must tell him to face up to the truth or leave you alone.

Well now, if some wrongs are matched only by the sorrow of repentance, we must get a clear picture of what we want when we ask a person to repent.

Repenting is a four-storied mountain. We must pass

through all four levels before we are finished. Let me name them.

THE LEVEL OF PERCEPTION

The first awakening moment dawns when you see your own action through another's eyes. You perceive that their feelings about what you did are true. You have reached the level of interpersonal perception.

You do not need to see every detail of your falling-out precisely the way they see it. You will probably never, even after a thousand explanations, agree on exactly how it all happened. No matter. You see that they are right when they say that what you did to them was mean and unfair and insufferable.

THE LEVEL OF FEELING

You move now from perception to pain. Here you *feel* the pain that you made someone else feel. You share the hurt that you inflicted.

You somehow enter another's soul and share his suffering. Once there, you feel as if you are out in the cold, barefoot in the snow, stuck for a while in the inner hell of your own deserved condemnation. The family name of this pain is "guilt."

THE LEVEL OF CONFESSION

When you can tell those you hurt that you realize what you did was intolerable and that you share their pain, you reach the level of confession. If they believe you, your separate sadnesses begin to melt into one.

When you confess *this* way, you do more than *admit* your blame. Criminals are sometimes trapped into admitting what they can no longer deny; lawyers call this a "confession," but it isn't what I am talking about. Terrorists break their necks to claim blame for the worst sorts of brutalities; but they do not confess in our sense of the word.

Confession is different, too, from spilling the beans. Celebrities are not confessing when they hire ghost writers to tell their private stories. Confession is not for payoffs; it is for healing.

When you confess to another person, you do not merely admit that you did something; you tell the person you hurt that you hurt too, with the very hurt that you hurt them with, and that you want terribly to be forgiven.

It is awesomely hard to confess to friends, I know—a lot easier to confess to God than to a wounded brother. And the deeper you hurt them, the harder it is to confess to them.

When you confess, you put yourself helpless in the hands of the person you wronged, trust him with your very self, bringing nothing with you but your hope for a sign of love. Confession is the rumbling of a crumbling heart.

THE LEVEL OF PROMISE

If you know and genuinely feel the wrongness of what you did, you also feel a passionate desire not to hurt again. So you make a promise.

Why should you expect anyone to take your confession seriously unless you promise that you do not intend again to foul your relationship with still more of the same unfair pain?

You can give no guarantee; the best of us go back on promises. But anyone who has been hurt should expect a sincere *intention*, at least.

These, then, are the four stories of the mountain of repentance: *perception, feeling, confession*, and *promise*.

It seems right that people who want you to forgive them should give you a signal that they repent.

Most of us who have read the story of the Prodigal Son feel good when the son says to his forgiving father, "I am not worthy." But try changing the scenario. See the son swaggering home and hear him say: "I've decided to do everybody a favor by coming back to my old place in the family circle." We will not have it that way. We want him to stick to the original script: "I don't deserve even to be a hired hand."

Take Marmelodov. Dostoevski tells us about him in *Crime and Punishment*.

Marmelodov was a wretched lush who ruined everyone who loved him. He pushed his angelic daughter Sonia out on the street to sell her body to keep him on the bottle. He stole grocery money from his long-suffering wife, Katerina.

But Marmelodov fully expected to be embraced in the end by the loving arms of a merciful God. Decent folk mocked his hopes, chided him, louse that he was, for presuming on the mercy of the Lord. Where did he get off, the most loathsome rat in the sewer, thinking that he could deserve a mansion in heaven prepared for him?

Ah, said Marmelodov, that is just the secret: he *knew* he didn't deserve it. He had had a vision in which God welcomed home all the prodigals of the world. " 'Come forth ye drunkards, come forth, ye weak ones, come forth, ye children of shame!' And we shall all . . . stand before him. And he will say to us, 'Ye are swine . . . but come ye also.' And the wise ones . . . will say, 'Oh, Lord, why dost thou receive these men?' And this is what the Lord will say to his critics: 'This is why I receive them, oh ye wise, this is why I receive them, oh ye of understanding, that not one of them believed himself to be worthy of this.' "

The art of getting back into fellowship after we have done someone dirt is knowing we don't belong there. We must *know* we are not worthy. And, like Marmelodov, we need to say so. If we are the ones who hurt someone, we should repent; repentance is the only honest entrée to forgiveness.

But supposing we are the ones who have *been* hurt. Must we *demand* repentance *before* we forgive the person who hurt us? Should we hold back on forgiving when the other one holds back on repentance?

God takes the tough line, it seems, from what we read in the Bible. When Jesus sent his disciples to tell

94

the world that God forgives, he also told them to ask people to *repent*. Following this lead, St. Peter put the cards on the table: "Repent so that your sins can be forgiven."

Why? Why do we have to repent when we want to be forgiven?

I don't believe God wants us to grovel just to give him the pleasure of watching us sweat.

My own guess is that God asks us to repent, not as a condition he needs, but as a condition *we* need. What God wants is not only that we *be* forgiven in *his* heart and mind, but that we should also *feel* forgiven in *our* heart and mind. He wants an *honest* coming together with his children. Asking for repentance was only a way of asking for *truthfulness*.

What about us mortals?

Should *we* waste our forgiving on someone who does not want it? Or admit he needs it? Pearls before swine? Pardon for the unrepentant? Let's have another look.

Realism, it seems to me, nudges us toward forgiving people who hurt us whether or not they repent for doing it.

For one thing, time does not let people stay near us forever. They may die before they have gotten around to repenting. But we need to forgive them anyway.

And, second, there is a matter of letting others take responsibility for themselves. We cannot *make* them repent; we cannot pull them back to us like a dog on a leash. Let them be responsible for staying away from us. But why should we let them keep us from healing ourselves?

So we need to forgive the unrepentant for our own sake. We need to forgive people who do not care if only so that we do not drown in our own misery. Let the other guy take care of himself.

I love a Jewish sentiment found in an ancient document called the *Testaments of the Twelve Patriarchs:* And "if a man sin against thee . . . if he repent and confess, forgive him. . . . But if he be shameless, and persisteth in his wrongdoing even so forgive him from the heart, and leave to God the avenging."

Leave the avenging to God—that, I think, is the way for us to cope with people who hurt us and do not seem to care.

The climax of forgiveness takes two, I know. But you can have the reality of forgiving without its climax. You do not always need a thing whole to enjoy it at all. A blossom has real beauty even if it never becomes a flower. A climb can be successful though we do not reach the summit. Forgiving is real even if it stops at the healing of the forgiver.

Should you sentence yourself to the escalator of hate simply because the person you need to forgive does not want your forgiveness?

Back to fundamentals! Forgiving is a process. One stage is the healing of the forgiver's memory. If the people you forgive want to stay where they are, let them. You can make a solo flight to freedom.

CHAPTER 8

Forgiving Ourselves

Do you dare release the person you are today from the shadow of the wrong you did yesterday?

Do you dare forgive yourself?

To forgive yourself takes high courage. Who are you, after all, to shake yourself free from the undeniable sins of your private history—as if what you once did has no bearing on who you are now?

Where do you get the right—let alone the cheek—to forgive yourself when other people would want you to crawl in shame if they really knew? How dare you?

The answer is that you get the right to forgive yourself only from the entitlements of love. And you dare forgive yourself only with the courage of love. Love is the ultimate source of both your right and your courage to ignore the indictment you level at yourself. When you live as if yesterday's wrong is irrelevant to how you feel about yourself today, you are gambling on a love that frees you even from self-condemnation.

But there must be truthfulness. Without honesty, self-forgiveness is psychological hocus-pocus. The rule is: we cannot really forgive ourselves unless we look at the failure in our past and call it by its right name.

We need honest judgment to keep us from self-indulging complacency.

Let me recall the four stages we pass through when we forgive someone else who hurt us: we hurt, we hate, we heal ourselves, and we come together again.

We all hurt ourselves. Unfairly, too, and sometimes deeply.

God knows the regrets we have for the foolish ways we cheat ourselves. I smoked cigarettes too long, and while I puffed away on my pack-a-day, I feared the time that I would say: you fool, you fool, dying before your time, and you have no one to blame but yourself. Then there are the opportunities spurned, disciplines rejected, and addictions hooked into—they all can haunt you with a guilty sense that you did yourself wrong.

But the hurt your heart cries hardest to forgive yourself for is the unfair harm you did to others.

The memory of a moment when you lied to someone who trusted you! The recollection of neglecting a child who depended on you. The time you turned away from somebody who called out to you for help! These are the memories, and thousands like them, that pierce us with honest judgment against ourselves.

We do not have to be bad persons to do bad things. If only bad people did bad things to other people we would live in a pretty good world. We hurt people by our bungling as much as we do by our vices.

And the more decent we are the more acutely we feel our pain for the unfair hurts we caused. Our pain becomes our hate. *The pain we cause other people becomes the hate we feel for ourselves. For having done them wrong*. We judge, we convict, and we sentence ourselves. Mostly in secret.

Some of us feel only a *passive* hatred for ourselves. We merely lack love's energy to bless ourselves. We cannot look in the looking glass and say: "What I see makes me glad to be alive." Our joy in being ourselves is choked by a passive hatred.

Others sink into *aggressive* hatred of themselves. They cut themselves to pieces with a fury of contempt. One part of them holds its nose and shoves the other part down a black hole of contempt. They are their own enemy. And sometimes, in the ultimate tragedy, their self-hatred is acted out in self-destruction.

Of course, your inner judge may be an unreasonable nag, accusing you falsely, and flailing you unfairly. On the other hand, your better self often sweeps real guilt under a carpet of complacency. You con yourself just to save yourself the pain of confrontation with your shadowy side.

In any case, you shouldn't trust your inner judge too far.

Still, he *is* your toughest critic, and you have to come to terms with him.

So let us move on *to love's daring response*.

What happens when you finally do forgive yourself?

When you forgive yourself, you rewrite your script. What you are in your present scene is not tied down to what you did in an earlier scene. The bad guy you played in Act One is eliminated and you play Act Two as a good guy.

You release yourself today from yesterday's scenario. You walk into tomorrow, guilt gone.

Again, the word that fits the case best is "irrelevance." Look back into your past, admit the ugly facts, and declare that they are irrelevant to your present. Irrelevant and immaterial! Your very own past has no bearing on your case. Or how you *feel* about it.

Such release does not come easy. The part of yourself who did the wrong walks with you wherever you go. A corner of your memory winks at you and says, "Nice try old chap, but we both know the scoundrel you really are, don't we?" It takes a miracle of love to get rid of the unforgiving inquisitor lurking in the shadows of your heart.

Perhaps nobody has understood the tortured route to self-forgiveness better than the Russian genius Dostoevski. In his novel *Crime and Punishment*, he portrayed the inner struggle of self-forgiveness in the soul of a murderer named Ilyon Raskolnikov.

Raskolnikov did something as evil as anyone can do. He brutally murdered a helpless woman, an old pawnbroker—a miserable woman to be sure, and miserly, and mean, but innocent still. His guilt was stupefying.

No soul can bear such guilt alone, not for long. Sooner or later one must tell. Raskolnikov found a girl, an angel, Sonia, and he confessed to her. He told her everything.

She persuaded him to admit everything to the police, and he finally did. He was sent to prison in Siberia.

The loving Sonia followed him there and waited for him to forgive himself so that he could find the freedom to accept her love.

Raskolnikov could not forgive himself. He tried to excuse himself instead.

He came to grief, he said, "through some decree of blind fate"; he was destined to kill the old woman. Besides, when you come right down to it was his act really *that* bad? Did not Napoleon do the same sort of thing and do they not build him monuments? In clever ways like this he excused himself by finding deep reasons why he was not to blame.

Raskolnikov did not *dare to be guilty*.

"Oh, how happy he would have been," wrote Dostoevski, "if he could have blamed himself! He could have borne anything then, even shame and disgrace."

Yet, now and then, Raskolnikov did get a glimpse of "the fundamental falsity in himself." He knew deep inside that he was lying to himself.

And finally it happened. How it happened he did not know. He flung himself at Sonia's feet and accepted her love. "He wept and threw his arms around her knees." He finally had the power to love. And his power to love revealed that the miracle had really happened; he had forgiven himself.

He forgave himself? For such a crime as cold-blooded murder? Yes. "Everything, even his crime, his sentence and imprisonment seemed to him now . . . an external strange fact *with which he had no concern.*"

Release! Release by a discovery that his terrible

past was irrelevant to who he was now and was going to be in the future. He was free from his own judgment and this was why he was free to love.

Raskolnikov stands out in staggering boldness to show us that even the worst of us can find the power to set ourselves free.

Finally, the climax of self-forgiving; it comes when we feel at one with ourselves again. The split is healed. The self inside of you, who condemned you so fiercely, embraces you now. You are whole, single; you have come together.

You are not being smug. You care very much that you once did a wrong. And you do not want to do it again. But you will not let your former wrong curse the person you are now. You take life in stride. You have let yourself come home.

It does not happen once and for all. The hate you felt comes back now and then, and you reject yourself for doing what you did. But then you come back to yourself again. And again. And again.

To forgive your own self—almost the ultimate miracle of healing!

But *how* can you pull it off?

The first thing you need is honesty. There is no way to forgive yourself without it. Candor—a mind ready to forego fakery and to face facts—this is the first piece of spiritual equipment you need.

Without candor you can only be complacent. And complacency is a counterfeit of forgiveness. Some people are superficial, there is no other word for it. Drawing on the top layer of their shallow wits, they pursue the unexamined life with unquestioning contentment, more like grazing cows than honest human beings.

The difference between a complacent person and a person who forgives himself is like the difference between a person who is high on cocaine and a person who has reason for being really happy.

Then *you need a clear head to make way for your forgiving heart.*

For instance, you need to see the difference between self-esteem and self-forgiveness.

You can gain esteem for yourself when you discover that you are estimable, that you are in fact worth esteeming. To esteem yourself is to feel in your deepest being that you are a superb gift very much worth wanting, God's own art form, and a creature of magnificent beauty.

Sometimes you gain self-esteem only after you come to terms with the bad hand you were dealt in life's game.

I know a man who has what is cruelly called the Elephant Man syndrome; a tough hand to play, but the only hand he has. He has learned to see the beautiful person he is beneath his thorny skin, and he esteems himself—*because* of what he is. Kim, on the other hand, is a beautiful adopted child whose birth-mother dealt her a genetic disease. Kim has chosen to accept herself as an incredibly splendid gift of God because of what she is, and in spite of the tough hand she was dealt.

Blessed are the self-esteemers, for they have seen the beauty of their own souls.

But *self-esteem* is *not the same as self-forgiveness*. You esteem yourself when you discover your own excellence. You forgive yourself after you discover your own faults. You esteem yourself for the good person you are. You forgive yourself for the bad things you did.

If you do not see the difference, you may shout a thousand bravos at yourself and never come to the moment of self-forgiving. So you need a clear head about what it is you are doing.

You also need courage. Forgiving yourself is love's ultimate daring.

The reason it takes high courage to forgive yourself lies partly with other people's attitudes toward self-forgivers. Self-righteous people do not want you to forgive yourself. They want you to walk forever under the black umbrella of permanent shame.

I understand these people; I am one of them. There is something inside me that wants a wrongdoer, especially a famous wrongdoer, to keep a low profile, to take the last place in line, to speak with a meek voice; I want him to grovel a little. Maybe a lot.

So, when you walk and talk like a person who has sliced your sinful past from your present sense of selfhood, you will need courage to face the self-righteous crowd.

Then *you need to be concrete*.

You drown in the bilge of your own condemnation for lack of specificity. You will almost always fail at self-forgiving when you refuse to be concrete about what you are forgiving yourself for.

Many of us try, for instance, to forgive ourselves for being the *sorts* of persons we are. We are ugly, or mean, or petty, or given to spouting off; or, on the other hand, we are too good, a patsy, everybody's compliant sucker, humble servant to all who want to get something out of us.

But people who try to forgive themselves for being wholesale failures are not humble at all; they are really so proud that they want to be gods. John Quincy Adams, not the greatest, but a very good President, could not forgive himself. "I have done nothing," he wrote in his diary. "My life has been spent in vain and idle aspirations, and in ceaseless rejected prayers that something should be the result of my existence beneficial to my own species." The last words spoken by the great jurist Hugo Grotius, the father of modern international law, on his deathbed, were: "I have accomplished nothing worthwhile in my life." Such people sound humble with their moans about being failures in life; but they are really crying because they had to settle for being merely human.

You must call your own bluff: precisely, what is it that you need forgiveness for? For being unfaithful to your spouse last year? Good, you can work on that. For being an evil sort of person? No, that is too much; you cannot swallow yourself whole.

Most of us can manage no more than one thing at a time. "Sufficient unto the day is the evil thereof," said Jesus. When we overload ourselves with dilated bags of undifferentiated guilt we are likely to sink into despair. The only way we can succeed as self-forgivers, free from the tyranny of a tender conscience, is to be concrete and to forgive ourselves for one thing at a time.

Finally, you need to confirm your outrageous act of self-forgiveness with a reckless act of love. How can you know for sure that you gambled with guilt and won unless you gamble your winnings on love?

"She loves much because she has been forgiven much"—this was Jesus' explanation for a woman who dared to barge into a dinner party uninvited, plunk herself at Jesus' feet, and pour out a small cascade of love.

Love is a signal that you have done it, that you have actually released the guilt that condemned you. You won't always know exactly when you have forgiven yourself. It is like reaching the top of a long hill on a highway—you may not be sure when you have reached level ground, but you can tell that you have passed the top when you step on the gas and the car spurts ahead. An act of love is like quick acceleration. A free act of love, to anyone at all, may signal to you that you do, after all, have the power that comes to anyone who is self-forgiving.

You can buy her a gift! Invite him to dinner! Visit someone who is sick! You can put your arms around a friend you never touched before! Write a letter of thanks. Or tell Dad that you love him. All ways of confirming that we performed the miracle of forgiving ourselves.

Yes, love gives you the right to forgive yourself. And it gives you the power as well. At least to begin. Healing may come slowly, but better a snail's pace than standing still, feet sunk in the cement of self-accusations.

To forgive yourself is to act out the mystery of one

person who is both forgiver and forgiven. You judge yourself: this is the division within you. You forgive yourself: this is the healing of the split.

That you should dare to heal yourself by this simple act is a signal to the world that God's love is a power within you.

CHAPTER 9

Forgiving Monsters

There are monsters who do such evils as ordinary people dare not dream of. They may be towering titans who trample whole populations. They may be crawling worms who seduce little children into prostitution. Whether giants or punks, they hurt people so badly that they may disqualify themselves forever from forgiveness by a fellow human being.

What makes their evil seem too awful for forgiveness? Sometimes it is the pointlessness of it—the gang on a drugged joy-ride that kills a child playing hopscotch on the sidewalk. Sometimes it is the unimaginable enormity of it—the Jim Jones who brainwashes a whole community to the point of mass suicide. There may be other reasons why any person could be too horrible to forgive; these are enough to make us wonder.

Are some people unforgivable? How can we tell?

There is at least one persuasive reason for leaving terrible evildoers unforgiven.

If we forgive the monstrous evils of the world, it is feared, we will shrink their horror. Forgiveness may reduce them so that a tolerant human society begins to swallow and digest evil while it gets on with business as usual.

Out of her passion for honesty, novelist Cynthia Ozick says that forgiving monsters "blurs over suffering and death. It drowns the past. It cultivates sensitivity toward the murderer at the price of sensitivity toward the victim."

Cynthia Ozick puts the matter precisely where it belongs: at the bar of honesty with those who suffer. But I honestly believe there is another way of looking at it.

Forgiving does not reduce evil. Forgiving great evil does not shave a millimeter from its monstrous size. There is no real forgiving unless there is first relentless exposure and honest judgment. When we forgive evil we do not excuse it, we do not tolerate it, we do not smother it. We look the evil full in the face, call it what it is, let its horror shock and stun and enrage us, and only then do we forgive it.

Besides, the greatness of evil is not simply a matter of *quantity*.

Pain is not measured only by the *number* of people who suffer it. If there are two people in a room, and one of them has a splitting headache, you would not double the amount of headache pain if the other person gets a headache too.

If you are betrayed, you feel *all by yourself* the pain that all the betrayals of human history bring into the world. We cannot add up the pain of a hundred betrayals any more than we can divide up the pain between the people betrayed. Each solitary victim feels the full measure of the betrayal even though a million people are also betrayed.

A woman who has been raped does not ask whether a man bad enough to rape one hundred women is forgivable. She asks whether she can forgive the man who raped *her*.

And if evil were measured in numbers, how would we know when a criminal has crossed the forgiveness zone? By instinct? Would we appoint a United Nations Commission on the forgivableness of atrocities? Maybe consult a panel of Harvard philosophers? Not on your life! Better consult anyone at all, anyone who has never gone to school, but who has been deeply hurt and later healed of unfair pain.

Besides, if we say that monsters are beyond forgiving, we give them a power they should never have.

Monsters who are too evil to be forgiven get a stranglehold on their victims; they can sentence their victims to a lifetime of unhealed pain. If they are unforgivable monsters, they are given power to keep their evil alive in the hearts of those who suffered most. We give them power to condemn their victims to live forever with the hurting memory of their painful pasts. We give the monsters the last word.

Another, final, irony is this: when we refuse to forgive monsters we give them exactly what they want.

Monsters do not want to be forgiven. They want to be left alone to vindicate themselves in the eyes of the world. Virtually every Nazi big-wig dreamed—even as he was convicted at Nuremberg—that one day Germans would build a statue in his honor.

The self-defeating upshot is: if we disqualify giants of evil from forgiveness, we are cruelest to their victims and we give the monsters exactly what they want.

Consider, from just one more point of view, how we defeat our own purpose when we say that a monster is too evil to be forgiven.

When we declare an evil person to be beyond the pale of forgiveness, we create a monster who does not even *need* to be forgiven—a monster is excused from judgment by the fact that he or she is beyond humanity. This is the paradox of making any human being *absolutely* evil.

Let us mull it over a little while—to make sure the point gets through.

Take Adolph Eichmann, for instance: a master-architect of the holocaust. Eichmann engineered an evil so horrendously huge that none of us has yet felt its full horror. Found guilty of crimes against humanity by an Israeli court, he was hanged in Jerusalem.

Was Eichmann forgivable?

Hannah Arendt went to Jerusalem to report on the Eichmann trial. She watched this man, listened to him, researched him, studied him, and then wrote a book that she called *Eichmann in Jerusalem: A Report on the Banality of Evil.*

Banality? Of *this* evil? Banality calls up words like stupid, trite, flat, vapid, empty, and boring. How could she talk this way of Eichmann and his monstrosities?

Arendt was *not* saying that the evil Eichmann did was not all that bad. She was trying to say that Eichmann was not superhuman, not even a superhuman monster; he was a stupid, boring, flat, ordinary man who used his human freedom to become a human tool of the Nazi machinery.

Some people were outraged by Dr. Arendt's words—the "banality of evil." But I ask whether they fell to another temptation. Did they superhumanize Eichmann's evil? Did they made Eichmann an evil god?

I think they superhumanized Eichmann's evil. Eichmann was made into a concentrated core of undiluted evil, an absolute version of evil's very essence, equal with the devil himself. Eichmann became an evil god, his humanness became a mere mask that covered the kind of pure evil that only gods can be or do.

By turning Eichmann into an unforgivable monster, we set him beyond human accountability, *beyond good and evil.* Nobody forgives the devil. Why not? It is because he is *beyond* the struggle between good and evil; he is only pure evil, and therefore we set him outside the possibility of being forgiven.

The paradox!

So we exterminate Eichmann. We swat him like a deadly mosquito. We shoot him down like a vicious beast prowling through our village. We do not judge him as a merely accountable human being, we liquidate him as a *non*human.

The truth of the matter is: very ordinary people do extraordinary evil. We need to judge them, surely, and forgive them, if we can, because they are responsible. And because we need to be healed.

If forgiving is a remedy for the wounds of a painful past, we cannot deny *any* human being the possibility of being forgiven lest we deny the victim the possibility of being healed through forgiving.

Love makes forgiving a creative violation of *all* the rules for keeping score.

But what of the victim's *ability* to forgive? *Can* the victim of monsters really forgive them? That is another, very different question.

The answer is not blowing in the winds for everyone to hear. It can only come straight from the heart of the person who, for some hellish moments or years, was brutalized by a monster. The answer cannot come from me, nor from anyone who is not a survivor of the evil that monsters have done. It can come only from those who have seen the monsters with their own eyes and felt the monsters' evil in their own lives.

Perhaps the answer of power cannot come from the mind. Perhaps it comes only from the pain-wracked heart. And, finally, from the heart possessed by hope.

CHAPTER 10

Forgiving God

There is an old, old story about a tailor who leaves his prayers and, on the way out of the synagogue, meets a rabbi.

"Well, and what have you been doing in the synagogue, Lev Ashram?" the rabbi asks.

"I was saying prayers, rabbi."

"Fine, and did you confess your sins?"

"Yes, rabbi, I confessed my little sins."

"Your little sins?"

"Yes, I confessed that I sometimes cut my cloth on the short side, that I cheat on a yard of wool by a couple of inches."

"You said that to God, Lev Ashram?"

"Yes, rabbi, and more. I said, 'Lord, I cheat on pieces of cloth; you let little babies die. But I am going to make you a deal. You forgive me my little sins and I'll forgive you your big ones."

The Jewish tailor grabbed hold of God and held him to account.

Rabbi Harold Kushner suffered the inexpressible pain of watching his son die of old age before he was fifteen. In his book *When Bad Things Happen to Good People,* he opens our heart's door again to this question: Where is God and what is he doing when decent people are hurt, deeply and unfairly? Kushner does not believe it is God's fault when bad things happen to us; we can't expect one God to handle *everything*. So we can excuse God. And yet he challenges us to forgive God anyway:

> Are you capable of forgiving . . . God . . . when he has let you down and disappointed you by permitting bad luck and sickness and cruelty in His world and permitting some of these things to happen to you?

You may react automatically: God cannot be blamed for anything, so he cannot be forgiven for anything. The Psalms say, "The Lord is just in all his ways, and kind in all his doings." Being God is never having to say you are sorry.

When it comes to God, our instinctive piety rushes to defend him against our own complaints.

Maybe so. But we should not smother the primal screams of those who feel as if God has left them dangling in the winds of pain. Would it bother God too much if we found our peace by forgiving him for the wrongs we suffer? What if we found a way to forgive him without blaming him? A special sort of forgiving for a special sort of relationship. Would he mind?

Let us try; let us talk a little, reverently but honestly, about forgiving God. Recall the four stages of forgiving? The first two are our *hurt* and our *hate*.

FIRST, THE HURT

Focus on hurts you feel are unfair and deep. Don't try to forgive God for not having made you smarter or more beautiful. Don't forgive him for not giving you wealthier parents with star-quality genes. Nobody gets everything in life.

And it stands to reason that you should not try to forgive God for lumps you give yourself. If you smoke two packs of cigarets a day for twenty years, you do not have to forgive God if you get lung cancer.

But sometimes we suffer a lot for no good reason, while folk of smaller virtue get along fine. One woman prays for ten years to have a child and never gets one;

112

a teenage girl playing around with sex skips off to an abortion clinic to get rid of what that woman wants more than anything else in life. One man obeys all the rules of good health and dies of a brain tumor at thirty-five; his friend smokes and drinks and grows a massive potbelly and lives to be eighty-five. A little help from God would have come in handy.

Sometimes God would have to do hardly anything at all.

Harry Angstrom, in John Updike's novel *Rabbit Run,* left the house in a huff one night; his wife Janice stayed home with the baby and got a little drunk. Janice gave the baby a bath. In the bathtub. But the baby's body was slippery with soap and Janice's mind was not managing her hands. She grabbed but she had trouble getting a good hold; she kept grabbing, but she could not find the right handles.

A contorted sense of horrible danger seized her confused mind, and then she knew "that the worst thing that has ever happened to any woman in the world has happened to her."

Harry came home several hours later and learned the terrible truth.

He went to the bathroom. The water was still in the tub, so he rolled up his sleeve and pulled up the stopper by jerking the chain that held it to the faucet.

Harry groaned: "how easy it was, yet in all his strength God did nothing. Just that little stopper to lift."

You can hear Harry's moan almost everywhere. The stoppers do not get pulled sometimes, and when they do not get pulled we feel naked against the icy blasts in the wintertime of our soul.

We need to look on the bright side, too, of course. Most of the time our babies do not drown in the bathtub. Our children get over the flu, ride their bikes home through busy traffic, evade the drug pushers, and escape child molesters. Mostly we do not get cancer; usually we tuck ourselves into bed and wake up in time to risk our lives in the next day's outing.

But when the bricks fall on us, we do not feel like balancing out our batting average by remembering all the happier days; we want to know why something could not have been done to prevent this one horrible hurt.

THEN, WE HATE GOD

It takes a tough soul, maybe somebody slightly mad, to hate God. Who is a big enough fool to wish God bad luck? Job did not have the bravado to follow his wife's advice: "Curse God, and die." Nor would I. Curse God? Not on your life!

But we do hate God sometimes. All of us, I think. On the sly.

If we dare not hate the Giver, we do dare hate his gifts. We hate his world. Or we hate ourselves. When we shut our eyes to every reason we have for being glad to be alive, when we resent good things that happen to our friends, when our hearts stifle every happy impulse, we are nurturing a passive hatred of God.

Maybe it takes an atheist to dare hate God head-on. I think of Graham Greene's Sarah, the woman in *The End of the Affair* who believed in God with such a frenzy that she just closed her eyes and jumped into faith. She loved people the way she believed God— with a trust that had no stops. But Sarah died too soon, unreasonably soon for someone who loved as well as she did and who had lately found a man who loved her too.

He hated God, her lover did, and he dared to throw his malice straight in God's face.

With your great schemes you can ruin our happiness like a harvester ruins a mouse's nest. I hate you, God, I hate you as though you existed.

True believers are more like the prophet Jeremiah. We do not dare to hate God, so we hate life instead.

114

When Jeremiah really felt let down by God, he turned his hatred on himself:

Cursed be the day on which I was born!
The day when my mother bore me, let it not be
    blessed.
Cursed be the man who brought the news to my
    father,
"A son is born to you," making him very glad.

Hating God's most precious gift is a believer's sneaky way to hate God.

You may hate him because you feel as if your most important friend has become your worst enemy. He could have pulled the rubber stopper, but he watched the baby drown. An ancient Jew said it a long time ago in the Book of Lamentations: "The Lord has become like an enemy, . . . he has multiplied . . . mourning and lamentation."

NEXT, WE DEFEND GOD

We plead his case against our own accusations.

Your believing mind wants to rush to God's defense against your frightening feelings of hate. And any thinking person can find good reasons why God does not pull the stopper that could have saved us from our troubles.

You can, if you think hard, look at your pains as flecks on a large screen of eternal harmony. God-haters take a cramped view of things; their pain blinds them to the large scene. Believers see things in perspective.

Walk into any large shopping plaza, and you will see the mish-mash of grey and white and black tiles that make up the floor. They don't seem to be arranged in any pattern at all. But get up on a balcony, high above the plaza, and look at the whole floor. Now the splendid mosaic comes to view. Your scrambled little corner looks good within the grand design.

You should not judge a Rembrandt painting by one darkish corner of a portrait. Step back. See the whole. The shadow only lets the light seem brighter.

So too with God's work; the dark shadows only underscore its shining glories. We will see—from the high place—that God makes all things fit together. All our pains will make his later mercies seem more tender.

There is a balm, I am sure, in this philosophical faith. It helps some people to believe that even the worst of their deep and unfair pains are really minor chords within God's great concerto.

But I would not say this to my neighbors across the street, who mourn for their twelve-year-old son Howard as he dies of a cancer that began in his testicles a few months ago and then worked up through his intestines where it intends to kill him soon. I dare not tell them that Howard's cancer will one day look good on the human canvas, like a shadow on a Rembrandt painting.

When I think I have found good reasons why we never need to forgive God, I think of Elie Wiesel. I think of him watching a little boy hang, almost but not quite dead, from a gallows at Auschwitz. In his unforgettable true story, *Night,* Wiesel tells us what he saw:

One day when we came back from work, we saw three gallows rearing up in the assembly place. . . . Three victims in chains—and one of them the little servant, the sad-eyed angel. . . .

The three victims (were) mounted together onto chairs.

The three necks were placed at the same moment within the nooses. . . .

At a sign . . . the three chairs tipped over.

Total silence throughout the camp. . . .

Then the march past began. The two adults were no longer alive. . . . But the third rope was still moving; being so light, the child was still alive.

For more than half an hour he stayed there, struggling between life and death, dying in slow agony under our eyes. And we had to look him full in the face.

Behind me, I heard [a] man asking:

"Where is God now?"

And I heard a voice within me answer him:

"Where is He? Here He is—He is hanging here on this gallows."

What voice did Wiesel hear inside his soul telling him where God was? Was it the voice of the brain? No. It was the voice of his heart!

The voice of the heart was the only voice he could listen to at that terrible moment. How cold, how cruel, any brain-contrived defense of God would have been!

Yet there are *some* things my mind tells me about God that seem reasonable in the face of my doubts. They do not prove that the hurts I feel all fit into a splendid pattern. But they may help me feel that God is my friend even when I suffer more than I deserve.

Let me speak of them.

Afterward, I will let my *heart* speak.

FIRST, I REALIZE THAT GOD GIVES ME THE KIND OF WORLD I WANT TO LIVE IN

I really want to be the sort of creature who can get hurt. I do not want to be an angel. I like being a body with nerve endings that give me pleasure when a woman touches them gently. But if she can give me pleasure by her tender touch, I must take the risk that she could hurt me with a brutal word.

He also made us free spirits in a world of free spirits. I like this part too. I would not change it for a world where people were nice to me because they had to be. But if I want to live among free people, I take the risk that some of them will sometimes do me wrong.

Pain comes with the territory. And I like being here. So why should I forgive God?

THEN, I THINK THAT GOD SUFFERS WITH ME

I do not feel much like forgiving someone for my suffering when he suffers as much as I do, maybe a lot more. When I complain to God: "Where were you when I needed you?" I think he says, in a still small voice, "I was there hurting with you."

Jesus wondered where God was when he was dying on the cross: "My God, My God, why have you let me down?"

But *had* God forsaken him? In retrospect, we know where God was while Jesus was hanging on the tree. God was not on leave of absence. He was in Jesus, suffering the pains of vulnerable love.

When I wonder where God is and what he is doing when I get hurt, one answer may be that he is *in me* and that my pains hurt him more than they hurt me. He is suffering with me, maybe to heal a small corner of his world through me. Maybe he suffers with us while he is working to bring about a new world where justice and peace embrace, and unfair pain is gone forever. This thought helps when I wonder if I should forgive God.

I BELIEVE THAT GOD FORGIVES

What does God do when bad people hurt innocent people for no good reason? One answer is: he forgives them.

I think of a conversation between two brothers, Ivan and Alyosha, in Dostoevski's novel *The Brothers Karamazov*. Ivan was an atheist. Alyosha was a believer. Ivan had seen some terrible things in his time; he had seen a little boy fed to a lord's wild dogs while his father and mother had to look on, all because the boy had eaten some fruit off the lord's trees. And a lot more. How can we believe that God could let bad people do such horrible things to innocent children?

Alyosha had no answer. He could think of only one thing to say. "There is one being who can forgive everybody everything because he shed his innocent blood for everyone and everything."

Did Alyosha really answer his brother? Not directly. But he did raise another question more serious than the one Ivan asked: Why should you forgive God when it is he who must forgive the people who are really responsible for doing the terrible things?

Something in me bends to Alyosha's answer.

These are some things I think about when I wonder where God is when people suffer. They help me feel him as a fellow-suffering friend of sufferers, not someone I need to forgive.

But they do not solve everything. The heart still wonders.

It helps to know that pain is a necessary shadow in the sunlit world in which I want to live. But does it have to hurt *so much?* It helps to know that God suffers with us when we suffer unfairly. But could he not heal it a *little faster?* It helps to know that God is willing to forgive people who hurt us. But could he not *prevent* some of the evil people from doing as much harm as they do?

I think we may need to forgive God after all. Now and then, but not often. Not for his sake. For ours!

So let us talk of healing ourselves as we forgive God.

Something happened to Doris and me once that forced me to come to terms with forgiving God. I am going to talk about it, though I know that what happened to us was not nearly as bad as a lot that happens to many, many other people; I mention it only because it was *our own* watershed time for forgiving God.

Doris and I had decided early on that we would have children as soon as I finished studies. But it didn't work. Doris did not get pregnant.

We went to fertility clinics everywhere we lived—in Amsterdam, in Oxford, in Illinois, in New Jersey, and in Grand Rapids, Michigan. We made love whenever the thermometer told us the time was at hand. We played our parts in the unromantic comedy of artificial insemination. We prayed in between.

And Doris finally did get pregnant, a little late in time, but really and roundly pregnant. What we wanted most was going to happen to us. Four months went by, and then another, and another. The seventh month began.

One night, getting towards ten, I was fixing crackers and cheese in the kitchen and Doris was muttering something sleepy from the sofa about getting herself to bed when, with the sentence only half out, she yelled my name. I knew instinctively that something bad was happening. It was. A dam had broken inside of Doris and she was flooding the davenport with an amniotic downpour.

Call the doctor. I fumbled my trembling index finger into the right holes of the telephone dial and finally got Ed Postma, our obstetrician, and heard from him a message I wanted terribly not to hear.

"Listen carefully. Put Doris in the car and get down to emergency. But I need to tell you something first so that you can tell Doris before you get here: the baby is going to be malformed, badly."

I got Doris wrapped in swaddling clothes and nestled her, legs bent high, into the back seat of our rusted-out red Plymouth sedan.

And I dropped the horrible reality like a horrid lump into her frightened mind.

Badly malformed.

Can you live with it? Yes, I think I can. Can you? I don't know.

Our doctor was waiting for us in the emergency room.

We got Doris admitted and wheeled into the space for women on their joyous passage to the wonder of life-giving.

After several hours, time enough for us to come to grips with what was happening to us, her intervals of pain signaled that the hour of deliverance had come. I carried my vacant terror to a little sitting room where a truck driver, ten years younger than I, was waiting for his wife to give him a third perfect offspring. "God, I am not ready for this."

A couple of hours later Ed Postma came in, green-smocked, face mask still hanging over his chin, with a grin on his face that looked obscene to me. But his words were wonderful to hear. "The baby is fine," he said. "We were mistaken. Everything seems to be OK. A boy. Come on, we'll have a look."

We had a look. Offspring of my loins, soul of my soul, flesh of my flesh, hair of my hair, he lay, body wrinkled, eyes, nose, mouth pushed into three inches of crimson face, fingers like wee spindlings wrapped into fists the size of two red marbles, and he screamed. I was what I wanted to be; the blood father of a normal man-child.

I drove home in a joyous delirium that comes from a belief that the best thing that could possibly happen to anyone had just happened to me. I got a few hours of sleep, woke up and made plans to call some friends with my good news.

Before I had a chance to call anybody, however, our pediatrician called me from the hospital. I knew from his inflection that the milk of God's mercy was suddenly turning sour. The baby was not breathing well. I should come.

I drove back to where I knew there would not be a second miracle.

While Doris was still in the hospital I buried the baby. Doris never had a chance to see what he looked like. She brought him alive into the world while I waited outside and I brought him dead into the ground while she waited inside.

Then I began to feel the hurt. The hurt was the loss of what we had waited for, for so long, and wanted more than we wanted anything else. But it was also the teasing meanness of the crazy game that made us dizzy with pain. Why, after the night of getting ready to love a deformed child; why, after the surprise that even doctors called a miracle; why, miracle done, was death the punch line? I felt as if I were the butt of a cruel divine joke.

Would I end up hating God? I knew I would never have the courage to bring my hate up front, where God could see it. I would turn my hate, as Jeremiah did, on life.

But we healed ourselves more quickly than we thought we could. I wasn't aware of it then, but I know now that what we did for healing was something like forgiving God.

We leaned on each other for strength; and we soon began together to feel a strange sense of our life's goodness in spite of this one rotten thing about it that had come upon us one cruel night when we felt we had a right to something very good. The feeling came to us; we did not arrive at it as a thinker finds his answer to an intellectual problem. We just sat there on her bed, and we cried, wondered, loved, grieved together, and, in our all-aloneness, hardly thought straight about anything at all.

We *felt together*, never wondering whether it hurt one of us more than the other, only sensing that we were together in our grief and our emptiness and our confusion. And that was good. Our life was good in our *shared* hurt!

In our strange euphoria about life's goodness, I felt God again as the giver, not the taker of life. As the God I know in the suffering Jesus, not a god who pointlessly makes us suffer.

I knew that I could not feel this goodness and also think that God took my child away. I knew my mind would forever say "I don't know" when my heart asked why little babies die. I heard my heart tell me that God was with us, "dying" a little along with our baby.

I understand no more today than I did then about how God was involved within the crazy game Doris and I had to play that March night. But I am sure that I shall never throw it up to him or remind him of the time he let us down.

Did I forgive God? In a way I suppose I did.

But there is a difference between forgiving God and forgiving an enemy. When you forgive your enemies, they may stay your enemies even after you forgive them. When you forgive God, you just live in the silence, and grope toward the goodness of life, and believe that, in spite of everything, he is your friend.

Part 3

HOW PEOPLE FORGIVE

Forgiving is love's revolution against life's unfairness. When we forgive, we ignore the normal laws that strap us to the natural law of getting even and, by the alchemy of love, we release ourselves from our own painful pasts.

We fly over a dues-paying morality in order to create a new future out of the past's unfairness. We free ourselves from the wrong that is locked into our private histories; we unshackle our spirits from malice; and, maybe, if we are lucky, we also restore a relationship that would otherwise be lost forever.

Forgiving is a miracle, however, that few of us have the magic to perform easily. Never underestimate the demands that forgiving puts on an average person's modest power to love. Some skeptics, when they heard Jesus forgive people, challenged: "Who can forgive sins, but God alone?" The English novelist Charles Williams remarked that forgiving is really a game; we can only play at it, he said, essentially we cannot do it.

Nobody seems to be born with much talent for forgiving. We all need to learn from scratch, and the learning almost always runs against the grain.

We talk a good forgiving line as long as somebody else needs to do it, but few of us have the heart for it while we are dangling from one end of a bond broken by somebody else's cruelty.

Yet, people *do* forgive—ordinary people, not saints—and they do heal themselves of terrible pain.

I invite you to see how ordinary people work out their own ways of forgiving. They do not have to be your ways, not in detail, certainly. But it may help to watch how other people do it. Don't expect gimmicks or techniques; look for signals and hints. Remember, nobody said it was going to be easy.

CHAPTER 11

Slowly

It takes time. A lot of time for some. Sometimes you struggle with it so long that you cannot remember the moment you finally did it; you just wake up one day and, on thinking about those you want to forgive, are a little shocked to realize you have already begun to forgive them. You know it because you find yourself wishing them well.

As a boy, C. S. Lewis, the British Christian scholar who wrote marvelous children's fantasies, was badly hurt by a bully who made a living as a teacher in an English public school. This sadist turned the lives of his boys into a living hell. Lewis could not forgive this teacher, not for most of his life, and being a failure at forgiving troubled him. But not long before he died, maybe just a few months, he wrote a letter to an American friend.

Dear Mary,
    . . . Do you know, only a few weeks ago I realized suddenly that I had at last forgiven the cruel schoolmaster who so darkened my child-hood. I'd been trying to do it for years; and like you, each time I thought I'd done it, I found, after a week or so it all had to be attempted over again. But this time I feel sure it is the real thing. . . .

Yours,
Jack

It was the real thing, no doubt. But maybe, if he had lived, Lewis would have had to do it a few more times. The hate habit is hard to break, harder than any, I think. And, as we do with other bad habits, we usually break it many times before we finally get rid of it altogether.

I joined two old friends recently in a lunch to commemorate the thirtieth anniversary of a great academic debacle. They were the heroes of the piece, professors at the seminary where I had been a student. We saw them then as young men with a dream, injecting a new vision into a bone-weary academic body. Others saw them as cocky threats to a great orthodox tradition. So, while the world outside knew little and cared less, they began a battle for the mind and heart of that school.

A classic struggle was joined between scholarly vitality and academic rigor mortis. Rigor mortis won. My friends were fired. And deeply hurt! Gallant all the way, but out on the street nonetheless.

Thirty years later, I raised the one question that I thought was worth asking my old teachers: "Have you forgiven the people who got you fired?"

One of them answered, "Come to think of it, I have been forgiving them for a long time. I slowly got it through my head that I needed forgiving as much as they did. What's more, it gradually dawned on me that the other men were about equally as decent and about as sneaky as I was. So about ten years ago I found myself wishing them well. We never became friends, but if our situations had been different we might have. So, I guess I have forgiven—and I think I've been forgiven. It took me a long time, too long, but I'm glad it's been done."

The worse you've been hurt the longer it takes to forgive. Minor bruises can be handled quickly. But when you've been sliced and diced inside your being, you'd better count on a longer process.

Sometimes we do it so slowly that we pass over the

line without realizing we have crossed it, as children pass from childhood to adulthood not knowing just when they crossed over.

Sometimes you seem to slide into forgiving, hardly noticing when you began to move or when you arrived. But after a long dry desert of trying, you gradually get a feeling that somewhere along the way you crossed the line between hating and forgiving.

At the beginning of the process, it helps to make a firm decision—one way or the other, fish or cut bait, here and now, and that's that—just to get going.

I remember a delicious hate I tasted a year or so ago that I would probably still be sucking on if I hadn't made a hard decision to spit it out. Let me tell you about it.

One warm June day, in midafternoon, a cop in our little town of Sierre Madre, hot with zeal to keep village pot smoking under control, brutalized my youngest son, John, in front of my own house. He was large, 250 pounds or so of vigorous lawman, and he threw all his violent bulk against my slender 140 pounder who, unknown to the officer, had a liver ailment that made hard physical contact a hazard to his life. In any case, the policeman roughed up John excessively and then charged him with resisting an officer.

The charge was quickly dismissed.

But I did not so quickly dismiss my bitterness. I took my anger down to city hall and tried to persuade the chief to rebuke the officer, just a bawling out, if you please, to help keep brute force in check. I offered signed statements by witnesses to the assault. But the chief of police in our peaceful village was not moved to criticize his own. He said he would look into the matter, but he never gave me reason to believe that he did. Case closed.

I did a secret dance of rage for several days, and the blue notes of anger gradually rose to cymbal-clanging hate. I controlled myself too well to knock anybody's block off, but I hated, passively at least; there was not an ounce of energy in me to wish the Sierra Madre police force well.

My hate almost became an instant addiction; I was infected by its virus, and I spread it to everyone who got close to me. To bring my hate to a spiritual crisis, I had a date coming up to preach a sermon on the grace of God at a Presbyterian church in Burbank.

Before Sunday came, I confided my feelings to a good friend, expecting her to add female indignation to my male malice; we would, I thought, sing a doleful duet of rage.

But she was on to me.

"Why don't you practice what you preach?"

I was trapped.

I had to decide then and there whether I really wanted to kick my hate before it got to be a habit. So I did. I opted out of hate.

But how could I make it work on the spot? I tried a technique that everything in my temperament resisted. I thought about how a priest gives instant absolution to a penitent, right off the bat, in the confessional booth. And I decided to give this cop absolution. It wasn't my style. I like to take my time when I solve my spiritual crises. But I tried it.

"Officer Milando, in the name of God I hereby forgive you. *Absolvo te*—go in peace." I said it out loud, at least six times.

Well, it worked enough to get me going anyway. I felt myself pry a couple of inches off my hate. And I was on my way.

A beginning. I am not finished with it yet. But I think that a clear-cut choice for forgiving was what I needed to set me in motion.

For some people, one definite decision is enough. For most of us, it is only a start on a long forgiving journey.

CHAPTER 12

With a Little Understanding

A little understanding makes forgiving a lot easier. If you understand *everything,* of course, you don't have to forgive at all. But it helps to understand *something* when forgiving comes very hard.

When we get hurt we are half-blinded by our pain. There is always more going on in an encounter with pain than meets the eye of somebody freshly hurt; it takes a while to see it. Even longer to understand it.

Sometimes, by understanding *some* of what was really going on inside the person who hurt you, you make forgiving a little bit easier for yourself, even though you still have to plow by hand through a thick crust of hurt and hate.

Careful, though; you are not going to understand *everything*. Those who hurt you did not really have to do it; they could have acted differently. To that extent, you will always be left with mystery; you can never fully understand evil *freely* chosen.

But if you can understand what might have influenced them, and understand a little bit of how they could have hurt you, you'll take a first step toward forgiving.

The hardest person for me—ever, in my whole life—to forgive was Mrs. Broutmeier. Mrs. Broutmeier lived in a yellow frame house across the street from the smallish house my father built with his own hands for us to live in just before I was born. This woman was unbelievably cruel to my mother and her memory has plagued me for years.

My parents shipped off third-class to the United States from Friesland, a province up in northernmost Holland, as soon as they were wed. My father lived just long enough to see five children born and to get his own house almost built on Amity Avenue in Muskegon, Michigan. Then he died, only thirty-three years old and hardly underway. I was the last of the five.

Left alone, with few skills and no money, my mother put bread on our table and clothes on our bodies by cleaning other people's houses and washing other people's clothes in a secondhand Maytag that broke down every other Monday.

On Amity, every house had its own splendid maple at the curb; too big around for climbing, they provided fine shade for sitting on the wooden swing that hung from the ceiling of each front porch. Our houses were all perpendicular to the street, none of your rambling ranches there: livingroom up front and a kitchen out back, with a dining room tucked in between them. You could shoot a rifle from the back stoop of the kitchen straight through the front door without hitting anything. Sometimes, if they were set just right, you could stand at your back door and look through your house all the way through the house across the street. The houses looked at each other, bay window to bay window, like poker players in a stare-down.

Our own house stood eyeball to eyeball with the Broutmeiers'.

I should explain that the Broutmeiers were our "betters." What made them "better" was partly that Mr. Broutmeier had a steady job and Mrs. Broutmeier stayed home and kept her children's noses clean. (You were a high-class kid in our neighborhood if your mother never let your nose get snotty.) But their "betterness" came out most plainly in the accent factor; they spoke English like real Americans. They were second-generation people; they had been around, they knew how to live, and, more than anything, they knew how to talk.

Mrs. Broutmeier, in all her true American betterness, became a monster. She had a co-monster next door, too, and the two of them set up a neighborhood CIA to keep an eye on the subversive goings-on at our house. She and her fellow monster drew straws at dusk every day to see which of them would report the delinquencies of her grubby kids to my mother as she came home from that day's scrubbing.

Once they both came across Amity to deliver to my mother the well-considered counsel of her betters that she should give her two youngest children—my brother Wesley and me—away as orphans, the reason being that my mother lacked the money and the savvy to care for us all in a proper manner. I remember getting word once that Mrs. Broutmeier had decreed that I should not cross Amity street to play with her children; I was exiled to the north side of the street on grounds of a dirty nose. It seemed to us, in fact, that the Broutmeiers had us staked out, night and day.

Mrs. Broutmeier and her confederate pressed the advantage of second-generation Americanism to the moral edge; they wore my mother down with shame. They got her to feel that it was a shameful thing for a woman with a brood of little children to let her husband die so young and an immoral thing to be talking to real Americans with a foreign accent on her tongue.

But my mother dipped her shame into a cup of heroic wrath. Deep down, where God's gift of dignity was simmering in her soul, she raged, she seethed. She was a goddess with fire in her bosom.

One Saturday night, done in, as if life had tied the terrible tiredness of all six working days in a bundle and given her one final blow, the latest Broutmeier slap at one of her children popped the safety valve on her fury.

We were, all six of us, in the kitchen, waiting for a pot of brown beans to finish baking, when, driven by the furies inside of her, she left the stove and strode head down, face red, fists tight, through the dining room, the livingroom, and out the front door. With apron strings fluttering behind her, she stalked across

Amity and up the Broutmeier front stoop to lay siege on the monster. The hosts of heaven never had a chance to stop her.

The five of us huddled around our bay window; we could see it all from there.

She pounded on the front door and, when Mrs. Broutmeier opened it a wedge, she pushed it aside and walked into the devil's lair. Face aflame, eyes brimming with tears, finger cocked straight at the shocked Broutmeier eyes, the widow Smedes launched a frenzied defense of her beloved brood.

Mrs. Broutmeier retreated to the dining room and took up a protected position on the other side of a round oak table with its blue Dutch teapot holding at the center. My mother used the table as a pulpit, pounding on it with her fist as she delivered her furious, inspired, but unrecorded prophecy against Broutmeier and on behalf of her own children. Mrs. Broutmeier sputtered something about the police, about calling them, and about being attacked by a woman gone crazy.

The word "crazy" seemed to bring my mother to her humiliated senses. Was she crazy? Maybe she was. She didn't know. If she was crazy, she was the more to be shamed. Better get out of there just in case. She left by the front door.

She walked, head still down, face white now, back across Amity, up our front porch, into the living room, past her children clustered at the window; she didn't look at us, didn't say anything to us, but strode straight ahead, through the dining room and kitchen, into the bathroom, and vomited. Then she wept. I do not remember when she came out or what she said to us when she did.

What I do remember is that we were sure Mrs. Broutmeier had done us all in. Our cup of shame was full. We would never have a friend in the neighborhood again.

I grew up hating Mrs. Broutmeier. I wanted her house to burn down. I hoped her children would fail in

134

school and get into a lot of trouble. I wanted them all to go to hell. My boyhood cup of aggressive hate was full.

Have I forgiven her?

I am still in the process of forgiving her. I enjoyed my hate too long, but I started to heal a long while ago and I am well on the way.

But I could never have forgiven her at all if I had not also tried to understand her.

I learned something about people who were born Americans, but from the womb of an immigrant. The Broutmeiers were second-generation immigrants with second-generation problems; they felt second-class to third-generation Americans, *their* "betters"—the "real" Americans. I learned how an ignorant woman with pride and ambition could think of a family like ours as a pool of inferiors in whose reflection she could see herself as almost equal to her own betters. I came to understand that our "inferiority" was a stool she stood on to lift herself to the level of the people a rung above her. In short, I came to see her as a weak, needy, and very silly woman who was using cruelty as a way of coping.

But I do not understand everything. I do not understand how Mrs. Broutmeier could freely choose to be so cruel. She was not driven by demons or dispatched by destiny to make my mother's life miserable. So even if I understand some of her circumstances, something about her cruelty is still beyond my grasp. She freely *chose* to hurt a decent woman, a neighbor who badly needed a friend, and such a choice is never to be completely understood.

Understanding your enemies helps bring them down to size. When we first feel the raw smart of an unfair assault, we draw a bloated caricature of that person— twice as large, twice as powerful, and twice as evil. Rotten to the core.

It also helps if you can understand *yourself* a little better, as the following story illustrates.

One night, right after Walter Cronkite had signed

off, Lena Brusbeck's husband Ben blurted out that he was in love with a woman half his age, had been for three years, and wanted to marry her.

What? For three years? The three years Lena had slept with him, nursed him, protected him from his nosey parents, kept track of his schedules, got him to work on time, made him look good and smell good, and, in general, made straight the highway for Ben and his trollop to get together? Those three years?

Lena's very virtue was her undoing. She trusted; he betrayed. She gave; he stole. She was true; he was a liar. She was faithful; he was faithless. Her only fault was the blindness of her pure love. Virtue had made a sucker of her.

Certain that any fool of a judge would see the rightness of her case, Lena hired a lawyer and sued for divorce. But Ben got himself the devil's own barrister, and he pulled Lena naked across the barbed wire of his inquisition and twisted her words into a testimony against herself. She began to look like the sharp-toothed culprit and Ben the guileless victim.

But the worse the lawyer made her look, the purer Lena felt.

She spent the next three years scourging her soul with replays of Ben's assault on her innocent devotion. She was insecure enough in her righteousness to risk some counseling with a view to getting psychological support for her malice. But her hate was undermined instead. As she found new insight into herself the bitter pleasure of her hate lost its edge. The long and short of it was that Lena began to see herself as a tarnished angel.

Ben did not deceive her; she deceived herself. She had really known all the while; but she did not dare to admit that to herself. The truth hurt too much, so she denied the plainest evidence. She wore the blinders of her own fear, more coward than fool. Her first eye-opener—insight into her dishonesty with her own self.

She also came to see that she had not been the self-giving lover she thought she had been. She really wanted security more than she wanted Ben, and she counted on Ben's commitment to give it to her. She bet everything on his morality. Ben was the sort of character who would stick with what he was stuck with. All she needed to do was remind him to be a good boy and she had him where she wanted him.

When she could see herself as she was—some good, some not so good—she made an opening for forgiveness to squeeze through.

Self-understanding reduced the act of forgiving to a minor miracle that even she could manage. She discovered herself wishing Ben well, and she felt free to be a more honest person the next time around.

With a little time, and a little more insight, we begin to see both ourselves and our enemies in humbler profiles. We are not really as innocent as we felt when we were first hurt. And we do not usually have a gigantic monster to forgive; we have a weak, needy, and somewhat stupid human being.

When you see your enemy and yourself in the weakness and silliness of the humanity you share, you will make the miracle of forgiving a little easier.

CHAPTER 13

In Confusion

Forgiving is wisdom's high art; most of us who work at it, however, are muddlers and bunglers. We usually move toward forgiving in the cross-currents of our confusion.

The confusion is not all our fault. The material we work with is often a mess. Exactly what happened is often unclear. Who did what to whom? How badly?

True, at the kernel of every falling-out, one person hurt another person. The bad guy does a bad thing and the good guy suffers for it. But tangled around that simple core of wrongful pain, we often find a skein of hurts and hates that is nearly impossible to unravel.

We are also hampered by a bog of *emotional* slough. To expect two people caught in mutual hate to sort out their pains is like asking a child to calculate the national debt. We often have to grope into forgiving through snarls of feeling as well as clogs of misunderstanding.

Just to show how decent people can stumble their way into forgiving through the dust of their homemade confusion, let me tell you about a sorry little drama in which I played a leading, but rather ridiculous role.

I had come to a new job in a new city where I had no friends, and I felt very insecure about my prospects for doing well. I knew only two people in town, Ted and Doreen, old acquaintances whom I hoped would become instant friends. I certainly needed them to.

Ted and Doreen had a chance to be a lot of help to

Doris and me almost as soon as we arrived. Doris landed in the hospital just as I got going at my work, and the children sometimes needed a place to go after school. Doreen came through generously and warmly. We were on our way to friendship, I thought.

Then, silently but effectively, Doreen closed the door. A freeze on friendship! A foreclosure on warmth!

What had I done? How had I offended? I went to Ted.

"Tell me what I did to hurt Doreen."

"Don't ask. Let well enough alone."

I couldn't let well enough alone. I had to get it all straightened out; I became a compulsive penitent. I asked again, got the same silence.

I wrote Doreen a letter, grieving for whatever pain I caused, asking forgiveness.

No answer. I didn't exist.

Now it was my turn. I was hurt, and my hurt quickly turned to hate. I was no longer the groveling penitent who had done someone wrong. Now I was the hurting victim; Doreen was doing *me* wrong. And I admit that sour resentment tasted better in my mouth than stale penitence.

But the situation was confused.

Which one of us really had to forgive the other and which of us needed to be forgiven? And if we both needed to forgive *and* be forgiven, who needed it most? Could we ever get it straightened out?

Out of molehills like this smart people are stupid enough to make mountains that only free forgivers can climb.

Forgiveness did come. It came by fits and starts, trickles, driblets of it seeping down the drains of our mutual resentments, but it did come.

Doreen and I moved toward forgiveness *as we made three shifts in our feelings* about our falling-out.

First, *we reduced our stakes*. In the early stage of our petty falling-out, we invested massive emotional resources in trivial offenses. We put our personal self-esteem on the block. We inflated the stakes beyond anything like their real worth. But time, that unsung colleague of love, gave us a chance to reduce our investments.

After all, what had Doreen done? And what had I done? Nothing much, probably; the impact on our feelings simply did not match the weight of each other's offenses. So we let each other's faults melt down to their real size. And our pain melted with our anger as we scaled down our mutual indictments.

Second, *we reduced what we expected from forgiveness*. As a matter of fact, Doreen and I no longer really wanted to be close friends. All we wanted from each other now was good will and a little respect. Once we understood that we did not *have* to be close friends after we forgave each other, that we did not *have* to come together the way I had wanted it earlier, our worried resentments receded as a spring flood slips back into the soft earth. Forgiveness was no longer a threat; we could forgive without feeling an obligation to embrace each other as good friends do. Being comfortable with each other in the same room, at the same table, at the same party was enough.

Third, *we reduced our desire for an even score*. We gave up trying to keep score of who did what to whom and how badly it hurt. We learned to leave the loose ends dangling, the scales off balance, to accept a score that neither of us could make come out even.

Full forgiving did not come in the twinkling of an eye. It came in bits and pieces with an unexpected meeting here, a gesture there, the exchange of a greeting, and a hint that better feelings were beginning to flow. We floundered into forgiving.

Not a triumph of the forgiver's art, I agree. But healing often comes on the wings of trivia. And the end is not always an ecstasy. We go to the same receptions and feel good wishing each other a Merry Christmas. Sometimes small mercies are tender enough.

We don't have to be virtuosos at the forgiving game to make it work.

CHAPTER 14

With Anger Left Over

Is there anger after forgiving?

Yes, often. It can't be helped.

Some people believe that they should not feel anger in their hearts once they forgive.

I do not agree. I think that anger and forgiving can live together in the same heart. You are not a failure at forgiving just because you are still angry that a painful wrong was done to you.

It is terribly unrealistic to expect a single act of forgiving to get rid of all angry feelings.

Anger is the executive power of human decency. If you do not get angry and stay angry when a bad thing happens, you lose a piece of your humanity.

Remember, you cannot erase the past, you can only heal the pain it has left behind.

When you are wronged, that wrong becomes an indestructible reality of your life. When you forgive, you heal your hate for the person who created that reality. But you do not change the facts. And you do not undo all of their consequences. The dead stay dead; the wounded are often crippled still. The reality of evil and its damage to human beings is not magically undone and it can still make us very mad.

A man does not *forget* that his father abused him as a child. A woman does not *forget* that her boss lied to her about her future in the company. You do not *forget* that a person you loved has taken cheap advantage of you and dropped you when the relationship was not paying off. I dare say that Jesus has not forgotten that a man named Judas betrayed him. And survivors of the holocaust do not forget the hell of that experience.

And when you do remember what happened, how can you remember except in anger?

Can you look back on the painful moment—or painful years—without a passionate, furious, aching longing that what hurt you so much had never happened? Some people probably can. But I don't think you should expect such placid escape from terrible memories. You can be angry still, and you can have your anger without hate.

Once you start on your forgiving journey, you will begin to lose the passion of malice. Malice goes while anger lingers on. When forgiving begins its liberating work, the malice that once hissed like white flame from an acetylene torch begins to fizzle out.

A man slowly finds himself wishing his ex-wife well in her new marriage. A father is surprised at how desperately he wants his rebellious daughter to be happy. We wish a blessing on the frail humanity of the person who hurt us, even if we were hurt unfairly and deeply.

What is happening? Malice is gradually fading, just as your head gradually stops pounding after you take three aspirin. You have anger without malice—a sign that your forgiving is real.

Anger minus malice gives hope. Malice, unrelieved, will gradually choke you. But anger can goad you to prevent the wrong from happening again. Malice keeps the pain alive and raw inside your feelings, anger pushes you with hope toward a better future.

There are three things you can do to drain the poison of malice while you use the energy of anger. They may be worth trying.

First, *express your malice*. Be specific, nail the object of your fury down. It doesn't help to let malice fester as an ugly glob of undirected misery. And it doesn't help to throw it at people, either. But you need to express it to somebody who can help you get rid of it. You can express it secretly to God, or to someone who represents God to you.

Then, you can *let God handle* those people you would like to manhandle in your hate. If they need teaching, let God teach them. If they need rescuing from their own stupidity, let God rescue them. If they need saving from their own crazy wickedness, let God save them. What you need is *healing* from the infection of malice left over from the open wounds they left in your life.

Finally, you can even *try a prayer* for the peace of the person you hate.

If you do, you may discover another secret of forgiving; you don't have to choke your anger, you only have to surrender your malice. For *your* sake. Malice is misery that needs healing. Anger is energy that needs direction. After malice, let anger do its reforming work. Forgiving and anger can be partners in a good cause.

CHAPTER 15

A Little at a Time

Wholesale forgiving is too much for anybody.

Not long ago a man named Arthur Fram came to me seeking a way to forgive his daughter, Becky, a fragile twenty-one-year old who had been suffering a fairly serious depression for a couple of years.

Becky stayed in bed until noon every morning. The rest of the day she lay on the couch in front of the television set watching soap operas and reruns of sitcoms. She got up once in a while during commercials, but only to stuff herself with junk food.

But there was more. Becky was surly and spiteful toward anyone who got close enough to join her at the television set. When Arthur offered to help her, or when he gingerly suggested that she help herself, she snarled at him like a cornered leopard. If anyone tactfully suggested psychological therapy, she shrieked in defiance against a family that accused her of being crazy.

In this way, Becky wrapped a thick blanket of rage and resentment around her, enveloping her whole family within it.

She needed help—lots of it, and soon.

But so did Arthur. He was ravaged by Becky's ferocious rejection of his longsuffering love. Because she spat poison at him as thanks for his fatherly care, he coiled a serpent of resentment around his fatherly heart. He felt cheated and he couldn't even the score.

Why should *he* have a daughter who had come of

age just in time to hate him with a vicious passion? Why should *he* have to explain to his successful friends, who bragged about their successful kids, why *his* daughter did nothing creative with her life? Why should his daughter play such a dirty trick on him?

Whose fault was it? Arthur had a hunch that it was his. Somewhere, somehow, he must have failed to be the kind of father he should have been. But he suppressed his hunch; he would not accept responsibility. "I'll be damned if I'm going to bear the guilt," he growled to himself—and growled it thirty times a day.

But bear it he did. And he was doubly angry at Becky for being the reason he had to feel such guilt when in another part of his mind he knew himself to be innocent.

Then he heard me talk about forgiving as a road to healing. He wondered whether he might have stumbled onto a quick cure for his aching heart.

He wanted to know how to forgive Becky.

"What do you want to forgive her for?" I asked. "Do you want to forgive her for suffering so much? Do you want to forgive her for hating herself? For condemning herself day and night because of the pain she knows she's causing you? Do you want to forgive her for being a person subject to depression?

"Must Becky be forgiven for letting you down by not being the classy young woman you need to impress your successful friends?"

Arthur was stunned. It was as though he had gone to a doctor for help and the doctor had assaulted him. But I was on to him; I recognized too much of myself in Arthur to let him pull a fast one on me.

Arthur was trying to use forgiveness as a quick and cheap nostrum for pains that forgiveness cannot cure. It cannot heal our narcissistic resentments toward people for not being all that we expect them to be. Nobody can really forgive people for *being* what they are. Forgiveness wasn't invented for such unfair maneuvering.

Arthur may be able to forgive Becky for cursing him

145

when he offered to take her to a therapist. He can probably forgive her for telling him she hated him at dinner the other night. In fact, he may have the power to forgive her for any of the *specific* things she *did* to help make his life miserable.

But he cannot forgive Becky for being a depressed person.

We overload the circuits of forgiveness when we try to forgive people for being burdens to our existence, or for not being the sort of people we want them to be. There are other means for coping with the threads of tragedy that are woven into the fabric of our lives. They go by such names as courage, empathy, patience, and hope. And God knows they come hard.

But I'm sure that I wouldn't have helped Arthur at all if I had encouraged him to think that he should—or even could—forgive his daughter for being the person she is, even though she has become the sad and needy center of his real, if self-centered, tragedy.

I believe that there is a natural law of forgiveness which requires a price from us when we try to forgive people for being what they are: *Those who forgive people for being what they are only increase their own pain.*

Pain compounds itself when we indulge ourselves with grandiose forgiving. The reason is simple to see. When we try—and fail, as we are bound to—to forgive someone for being what he is, resentment is added to resentment. We blame *him* for our failure to forgive him, as well as for wronging us.

We also end up feeling sorrier for ourselves than we did before, and guiltier too, because now, besides everything else, we are ashamed of ourselves for not being able to forgive. Our pain feeds on itself. It grows like an invisible carcinoma.

The long and short of what I've been saying is that the forgiving that heals focuses on what people *do,* not on what people *are.* The healing art of forgiving has to be practiced a little at a time—for most people anyway.

146

Ordinary people forgive best if they go at it in bits and pieces, and for specific acts. They bog down if they try to forgive people in the grand manner, because wholesale forgiving is almost always fake. Forgiving anything at all is a minor miracle; forgiving *carte blanche* is silly. Nobody can do it. Except God.

And the first rule for mere human beings in the forgiving game is to remember that we are not God.

CHAPTER 16

Freely, or Not at All

We are never so free as when we reach back into our past and forgive a person who caused us pain.

No one can be forced to forgive. No one forgives by blind instinct. Nor can anyone truly forgive out of duty. We stretch ourselves beyond the call of duty and the push of instinct into the lively sport of personal freedom when we genuinely forgive a person who did us wrong.

How silly, then, for a parent to nag at a daughter to forgive her brother for reading her diary and tattling about the secrets he found there. How futile, too, for a preacher to wheedle his congregation into forgiving their enemies by threats of judgment against unforgiving spirits.

The parent who nags and the preacher who wheedles are using a tactic that cannot work. We forgive freely or we do not really forgive at all.

We are not forgiving freely when we are driven to forgive by some inner need to control the person we forgive. Manipulating through forgiving only makes matters worse. But a lot of people try it.

There are three kinds of manipulative forgivers.

Trigger-happy forgivers fire off forgiveness at a moment's notice. Every time someone causes them some puny inconvenience, they clobber that person with punishing magnanimity.

If you are half an hour late for an appointment with

Joe, he forgives you before you can explain that a long distance phone call came just as you were leaving home. If you do not remember Fran's birthday, she forgives you with the gravity of a judge issuing a death sentence. If Teresa's son does not have his room cleaned, she forgives him without asking for an explanation.

The trigger-happy forgiver forgives the way an old boxer shoots out a left when he sees a twitch in his opponent's eye.

Stung by such indiscriminate forgiving, you may want to say: "But I do not need to be forgiven for this; I did not do anything bad enough to deserve your guilt-loaded forgiving." But you are trapped. The trigger-happy forgiver needs to be in control, so he intimidates through forgiveness.

Then there is *the stalking forgiver,* who sniffs out guilt and tracks it down, stalking it, like a hound dog on the trail of a rabbit. These forgiving sleuths want to find the culprits, tag them as wrongdoers, and then slap them with forgiveness.

Stan Hackley is a stalking forgiver. Stan is in charge of an office where keeping accurate records is of the essence. He walks in the valley of the shadow of fear, lest someone upstairs catch his office in a computer error. But there are ten people in his office who feed the computer at least once a day. He cannot control the diet, and the law of human fallibility decrees that, now and then, one of the ten will offer the wrong menu. When that happens, Stan the manager becomes Stan the stalker. He goes on a furtive hunt, poking for clues, uncloaking the culprit.

Stan wants tension, tears, grinding teeth.

Of course he always forgives. But his forgiving leaves judgment and shame in its backwash. He forgives and runs, leaving resentment circling through the office like summer heat blown around by a ceiling fan.

We also have the *entrappers,* who set people up to do the very thing they need to be forgiven for. Entrappers trap, forgive, and then drive their victims back to do the same thing again—so that they can be forgiven again.

Irma Walcort is an entrapper. She has forgiven her husband Clint at least a thousand times. But each time she forgives, she digs Clint's hole a foot deeper, and shoves him into it again.

Clint is a drunk. He does most of his drinking in the late afternoon, out of Irma's sight. Then he comes home, grunts, flops on the sofa, and sleeps the long evening away.

But on weekends he drinks early, and, by five o'clock Saturday afternoon, at the crescendo of a yelling brawl, he takes a few swats at Irma. He never remembers on Sunday morning. But Irma always remembers.

Like a burned-out priest reciting a Sunday morning liturgy, she snarls back to him all the rotten things he had said the day before, shows him a bruise or two, assures him that, beyond all doubt, he is considerably less than a worm, and then, with the inevitability of a closing commercial, she forgives him. She always forgives. She "forgives" the way a typist slams the carriage back at the end of a line.

Each time Irma forgives him, Clint is reminded that he is the worst louse ever to crawl through the crevices of humanity. The least he can do in response is to punish himself.

How does a lush smite himself? Why he gets drunk, of course. So that he can be thumped and smitten by Irma again, just as he deserves. And be forgiven again.

Loaded with contempt, Irma's forgiving is a cage in which she keeps her tippling husband where she wants him. It is the way of the manipulating forgiver.

To set anyone free, forgiving must be freely given—an act of free love, not a devious power play. Forced forgiving makes matters worse for everybody.

A major ingredient in free forgiving is respect for the person being forgiven. This person is a magnificent creature. You do not forgive your pet dog; you do not forgive your personal computer; you forgive only a superb being called a person. In practice, respect means that you let a person do whatever he or she wants to do with your forgiving.

You forgive in freedom only when you give other people freedom—to do what you don't want them to do at all, if they so choose. Anything less than the gift of freedom is control through forgiving manipulation.

If you try to manipulate people into your contrived version of a happy ending, you are not forgiving freely. And you are not really forgiving at all.

Only if you respect them enough to let them be responsible for what they do with your forgiveness will your forgiving be genuine. It is the risk one always takes in the forgiving game.

A free act is always a risk, one way or the other. Forgiving, above all, is one of freedom's biggest risks. But there is no genuine forgiving any other way.

CHAPTER 17

With a Fundamental Feeling

Ruth has been trying to forgive her mother for years. God knows it is hard to do. She knew early on that her mother never wanted her. She cannot remember ever being held in her mother's arms; as far as she knows, she was never cuddled, never tucked in bed, never kissed. What she does remember is being handed a lot of very expensive toys at a stiff arm's length.

When she was eight, her parents' marriage fell apart; her mother wanted a divorce. But there was Ruth, what would become of little Ruth? So, for the sake of a child she did not want, she hung on with a man she did not love. But she only resented Ruth more for burdening her twice—first with herself and then with her father.

Ruth, in her turn, hates her mother, who locked her out of family love as if she were an enemy alien. She has hated her mother so terribly long. All these years—the hound of her hate always growling in the bottom of her heart! She wishes her mother would die and let her forget, but she knows that her hate will outlive her mother.

Ruth's hate for her mother doesn't stop there—it has a hook in it that catches Ruth herself. In her heart of hearts she feels as if her mother was right about her from the start, that she probably was never worth loving. So she hates herself as much as she hates her mother.

How can Ruth break through the matted tangle of

hate that both binds her to and alienates her from her mother?

I do not think that Ruth will ever forgive her mother or herself until she feels forgiven herself. Coming to terms with the pain of her mother's guilt must follow the pain of coming to terms with her own. When she finally feels forgiven, fully and unconditionally forgiven, she will be free to forgive herself. And in forgiving herself, she will find freedom to forgive her mother.

What is it like to feel forgiven?

Forgiveness is fundamental to every other good feeling.

Try other sorts of delightful feelings and compare them with the feeling of being forgiven. Think of the feeling you have when you finally manage to do what you have been trying to do forever: "I did it! I did it!" The feeling is triumphant. Think of the feeling of making love with someone you really love. Or even the feeling of relief at seeing a familiar landmark after you've been lost and almost out of gas. These are all jubilant feelings, but none of them is fundamental. They do not make or break our joy.

But the fundamental feeling makes a difference to everything.

You feel forgiven at the ground floor of your being, where everything else rests. It is a feeling of total acceptance, a feeling lodged in your deepest self, a feeling that no bad thing you do can take away. You feel totally affirmed, totally loved, totally received. Your entire being is rested because you feel that nothing can separate you from the source of love, even though you cannot do enough good things to earn your right to be there. You know that nothing can really hurt you now.

This fundamental feeling happens *to* you. It comes as you are open to it. You cannot create it; you can only be receptive to it.

But you can *close* yourself to it. How?

One sure way of missing out on the fundamental

feeling is to worry too much about being a spiritual success.

We all want badly to have a place in the sun, nestled securely alongside the lucky people who have made it and who think very well of themselves for succeeding so well. We want to walk straight, heads high, in the well-earned sense of our own conspicuous worth. Of course, why not?

But sometimes we need to look at ourselves more honestly.

We do well sometimes to follow our feelings into the darker regions of our lives where we are neither very pretty nor very pure. We are a mixed breed, shadow and light, weak and strong, foul and clean, hate and love, all at the same time. Our middle name is *ambiguity*. Admitting this fundamental ambiguity opens us to the fundamental feeling of being forgiven.

Obsession with spiritual success can take you on idiotic detours around the fundamental feeling. I know a man who needs to be good so badly that he cannot face up to the puniest fault. He often groans about being a poor, poor sinner—always in gorgeous generalities, and always as a trick to get people to reassure him of his unusual virtue. But when his wife complains that he forgot to take out the garbage, he is ready to hire a criminal lawyer to defend himself against her indictment.

Why? The reason is simple: his passion to be a spiritual success will not let him fail at anything at all. He needs to be terribly good because he is scared to death of being the least bit bad. And he loses his chances at the fundamental feeling of being forgiven.

Let me speak for myself. When I am most anxious about my personal worth I become an armed guard of my ego's imperial highness. If someone assaults my self-esteem, I call up all my reserves to defend myself. I get rigid, grim, frightened; I am poised for attack.

I cannot allow myself to accept the feeling of being forgiven.

But in some awful hours of emptiness, when I knew that I could not win my case by defending my virtue, I have emerged feeling forgiven—and free and joyful and hopeful as well. I was free to forgive. Liberated by the fundamental freedom of being forgiven.

My favorite story of the freedom to forgive is the one Corrie Ten Boom tells about herself. Corrie was liberated from a Nazi concentration camp a few days after the Allies conquered Germany. It took longer to be liberated from her simmering hate. But she set out on the forgiving journey through her remembered pain and kept traveling until she arrived at the place where she forgave even the Nazis who had dehumanized her life in the camps.

In forgiving, she believed she had discovered the only power that could heal the history of hurt and hate for the people of Europe. So she preached the possibilities of forgiveness. She preached it in Holland, in France, and then in Germany, too. In Munich one Sunday she preached forgiving, preached it to all those German people who were so eager to be forgiven.

Outside, after the service was over, a major drama of the human spirit unfolded. A man walked over to her; he reached out his hand to her, expecting her to take it. "Ja, Fraulein Ten Boom, I am so glad that Jesus forgives us all of our sin, just as you say."

Corrie knew him. She remembered how she was forced to take showers, with other women prisoners, while this beast looked on, a leering, mocking "superman," guarding helpless naked women. Corrie remembered. He put his hand close to her. Her own hand froze at her side.

She could not forgive. She was stunned and terrified by her own weakness. What could she do, she who had been so sure that she had overcome the deep hurt and the desperate hate and had arrived at forgiving, what could she do now that she was confronted by a man she could not forgive?

She prayed. "Jesus, I can't forgive this man. For-

155

give me." At once, in some wonderful way that she was not prepared for, she felt forgiven. Forgiven for not forgiving.

At that moment—in the power of the fundamental feeling—her hand went up, took the hand of her enemy, and released him. In her heart she freed him from his terrible past. And she freed herself from hers.

The linkage between feeling forgiven and the power to forgive is the key to everything else.

Let me get back to my friend Ruth, the gifted woman who has suffered so long because she cannot forgive her mother. Ruth cannot forgive her mother because she does not feel forgiven herself.

Her freedom to forgive must come from a fundamental feeling of personal freedom from any and all condemnation, her own or God's or anyone else's. The fundamental feeling has no soil for hate to grow in, no nourishment for hate to feed on; when we experience the fundamental feeling, hate dies a natural death, and when hate dies we are free to forgive.

Do you remember Roger Sewall? Roger was the young man who was killed so cruelly by a hit-and-run driver.

Roger's mother, Phyllis, poured some of her pain into a diary, to help herself get through her terrible tangle of anger while she awaited the trial of the man who killed her son. She let me read her diary and allowed me to share what she wrote in it.

First, she reveals her hurt, and her hate.

"I don't know how I feel. I'm still mad. I'm mad at [Charid] for being on drugs . . . I want him to hurt. I want him to suffer for his guilt and feel our pain. I want him to have years of tortured dreams and sleepless nights. . . . God, I don't want to forgive him. . . ."

But Phyllis is a deeply spiritual person, and she could not feel her hate without feeling a need within herself. Moved by her own need, she approaches the edge of the fundamental feeling.

"What foolish children we are. . . . We keep turning

away . . . yet you reach out . . . and you say—I forgive you."

Now she claims it.

"I . . . receive . . . receive the forgiveness you have held out for us since the day *your* son died."

But she struggles a while longer.

"Can I forgive like that? No. I can't. . . . Help me God. Help me . . . to say . . ."

She couldn't finish the sentence; she couldn't write, "I forgive."

A few months later. Tears and anger later. In the power that comes from life's fundamental feeling, she finished the struggle.

"I forgive Sid Charid."

And she really did.

I don't know whether Phyllis's act ever touched the life of the man she forgave. I don't know whether he will ever forgive himself. What I do know is that when she forgave the man who killed her son, Phyllis began her own journey into healing. Maybe she has had to begin again, many times, but she is on the way.

Part 4

WHY FORGIVE?

There is a lot to be said for *not* forgiving people who have done us wrong. Why should people cut and thrust their way through our lives, leaving us bleeding in their wake, and then expect us to forgive everything and act as if nothing went wrong?

Forgiving *is* an outrage against straight-line dues-paying morality. "A beggar's refuge," George Bernard Shaw called it. And anyone who preaches the beauty of forgiveness should get it through his head that what he urges us to do goes against the grain of any decent person's yen for a fair deal.

We must face up to the skeptic's suspicion that forgiving is really a religious trick to seduce hurting people into putting up with wrongs they do not deserve.

Remember that we are talking about forgiving things that we feel are insufferable. We are not talking about the petty pains in the neck that we inevitably suffer in the human crush.

We are talking about forgiving people who have wronged us, hurt us, deeply and unfairly, and left us feeling lower than any human being in God's image should ever feel.

We must listen to the voices that cry out against forgiving such people indiscriminately.

If we hear these voices clearly, we will recognize in them an echo coming from our own hearts.

For the honest heart is outraged by cheap nostrums for unfair hurts; it does not want to forgive at all, if forgiving leaves the victim exposed and encourages the wrongdoer to hurt again.

So we shall ask: Why forgive?

And we shall answer: because forgiving is the *only* way we have to a better fairness in our unfair world; it is love's unexpected revolution against unfair pain and it alone offers strong hope for healing the hurts we so unfairly feel.

Let us go on, then, so that you can test the fairness of forgiving on the touchstone of your own heart.

CHAPTER 18

Forgiving Makes Life Fairer

Did Shylock have a case? He is, as all villain haters know, the classic unforgiver. But who looks at the business from Shylock's point of view?

We find Shylock in Shakespeare's *Merchant of Venice;* he had been kicked around, badly, and for no good reason. Listen to his complaint. "Antonio," he said,

> hath disgraced me . . .
> Laughed at my losses,
> Mocked my gains,
> Scorned my nation,
> Thwarted my bargains,
> Cooled my friends,
> Heated mine enemies.

And for what? Why did Antonio rub Shylock's face in the muck? Had Shylock done him wrong? Were there scores to settle? No, Antonio was spurred only by the evil spirit of anti-Semitism. Shylock was brutalized only because he was a Jew.

Why, then, should Shylock forgive Antonio as if nothing had happened between them? He asked for no more than he had coming. Antonio had made a bargain. Let the wrongdoer pay his dues. One pound of flesh please! As promised.

Shylock's simple-minded sense of fairness dimmed his wits. It did not take a genius to turn the tables on him: let him have one pound, not an ounce more, and only flesh, not a drop of blood. The Gentiles won the game. But our question is not whether Shylock was smart; it is whether his case was just.

I bring up Shylock only to raise the question of fairness in forgiving.

Simon Wiesenthal tells another sort of story we must hear at all costs; this story of his own terrible crisis of forgiveness in a concentration camp forces us to tremble a little as he asks again whether forgiving is really fair. Wiesenthal was the very opposite of a vengeful Shylock smacking his lips over the pound of flesh that was coming to him. He was a decent person, an architect by profession, caught in the Nazi claws, hoping for no more than to survive the holocaust, and hardly daring to hope for that much.

We find him one afternoon in a Polish concentration camp. Wiesenthal had been assigned that day to clean rubbish out of a hospital that the Germans had improvised for wounded soldiers carried in from the Eastern Front. A nurse walked over to him, out of nowhere, took his arm, ordered him to come with her, and led him upstairs, along a row of stinking wounded, to the side of a bed where a young soldier, his head wrapped in yellow, pus-stained bandages, was dying. He was maybe twenty-two, an SS Trooper.

The soldier, whose name was Karl, reached out and grabbed Wiesenthal's hand, clamped it as if he feared Wiesenthal would run away. He told Wiesenthal that he had to speak to a Jew. He had to confess the terrible things he had done so that he could be forgiven. Or he could not die in peace.

What had he done? He was fighting in a Russian village where a few hundred Jewish people had been rounded up. His group was ordered to plant full cans of gasoline in a certain house. Then they marched about two hundred people into the house, crammed them in until they could hardly move. Next they threw grenades through the windows to set the house on fire. The soldiers were ordered to shoot anyone who tried to jump out of a window.

The young soldier recalled, "Behind the window of

the second floor, I saw a man with a small child in his arms. His clothing was alight. By his side stood a woman, doubtless the mother of the child. With his free hand the man covered the child's eyes—then he jumped into the street. Seconds later the mother followed. We shot . . . Oh, God . . . I shall never forget it—it haunts me."

The young man paused and then said, "I know that what I have told you is terrible. I have longed to talk about it to a Jew and beg forgiveness from him. I know that what I am asking is almost too much, but without your answer I cannot die in peace."

Silence! The sun was high in heaven. God was somewhere. But here, two strangers were all by themselves, caught in the crisis of forgiveness. A member of the super race begged to be forgiven by a member of the condemned race.

Wiesenthal tells us what he did. "I stood up and looked in his direction, at his folded hands. At last I made up my mind and without a word I left the room." The German went to God unforgiven by man.

Wiesenthal survived the concentration camp. But he could not forget the SS trooper. He wondered, troubled, for a long time whether he should have forgiven the soldier. He told the story in his book *The Sunflower*, and ended it with an awful question for every reader: "What would you have done?"

I do not know what I would have done. I can never be sure how I would act in someone else's crisis. I only want to let his story compel us to consider well the outrageous thing we do when we urge anyone, including ourselves, to forgive someone.

Would it have been right for Wiesenthal to forgive? Or would it have been wrong?

Thirty-two distinguished people wrote their answers to Wiesenthal. Most of them echoed Josek, a fellow prisoner, who said to Wiesenthal:

You would have had no right to forgive him in the name of people who had not authorized you to do so. What people have done to you, yourself, you can, if you like, forgive and forget. That is your own affair. But it would have been a terrible sin to burden your conscience with other people's suffering.

A terrible sin to forgive! Why? Because no one may free a criminal's conscience unless he has been the criminal's victim.

But we must not let Wiesenthal's fairness to other victims keep us from asking the question of fairness to the SS trooper and to Wiesenthal himself.

A few writers came out with it: the SS trooper did not deserve forgiveness. Philosopher Herbert Marcuse said what one suspects was on the minds of most people.

One cannot, and should not go around happily killing and torturing and then, when the moment has come, simply ask, and receive forgiveness.

But no one else put the case against forgiving with the passion of novelist Cynthia Ozick:

Often we are asked to think this way: vengeance brutalizes, forgiveness refines. But the opposite can be true. The rabbis said, "Whoever is merciful to the cruel will end by being indifferent to the innocent." Forgiveness can brutalize . . . The face of forgiveness is mild, but how stony to the slaughtered . . . Let the SS man die unshriven. Let him go to hell.

Why *should* he die in peace? Why *should* he be released from his sin by a Jew's word? Why should anyone anywhere forgive this murderer and thus let him go free as if he had never pulled a trigger? Did he not *deserve* to die unforgiven?

Would it have been fair to Wiesenthal himself? He, too, had been awesomely wronged. Here he was, a hugely moral person, locked in a concentration camp, doomed to die with all the others. The Nazis left him with almost nothing; eighty-nine of his relatives were killed. Now, in one unexpected moment, he had the fate of a Nazi in his hands. Why should he not slice the super-race with the cutting edge of his silent contempt? Would he not have done *himself* a terrible injustice if he had spoken gentle words of forgiveness to the German?

Some people do not need a story like Wiesenthal's to tell them forgiving is unfair. They have felt the unfairness inside themselves, in the smaller fires of their own soul's furnace.

Take Jane Graafschap, for example. Jane and her husband, Ralph, had finally brought their three children through the crazy maze of adolescence, and gently pushed them out of the house. Jane was glad they had flown the coop; finally she was going to have a life of her own, get back on her own track and make something of herself.

But a family tragedy stopped her. Ralph's younger brother and his wife were killed in a car crash, and left three children, ages eight, ten and twelve, all by themselves. Ralph had a strong sense of duty; he knew that it was his sacred calling to take his brother's orphaned children in. Jane was too compassionate or too tired to disagree, she never did know which. She took them in, not for a month, but for the duration. As for Ralph, he was gone a lot, a traveling man, on the road, making deals. Nine years groan by. Two of the kids are gone; the only one still home is seventeen, his mind bent slightly out of shape but functional. In a few years Jane and Ralph would be home free.

Not quite. Jane's body had gotten a little lumpy by this time, while Ralph's secretary, Sue, was a dazzler; besides, Sue really understood his large male needs. How could he help falling in love? He and Sue knew that their love was too true to be denied and too powerful to be resisted. So, Ralph divorced Jane and he married Sue.

Ralph and Sue were very happy, and they dunked their happiness in a warm religious froth; their convivial, accepting church celebrated their new-found joy with them. They were kept afloat in togetherness by their affirming Christian community. But Ralph needed one more stroke of acceptance. So he called Jane to ask her to forgive him, and be glad with him that he was finally a happy man. "I want you to bless me," he said.

"I want you to go to hell," she replied. What? Forgive? Throw away the only power she had—the strength of her hate, the energy of her contempt? Her contempt was her power, her dignity, her self-esteem. It was unfair to ask her to forgive. The least the louse deserved was a steady stream of her scorn.

When we urge people to forgive, are we asking them to suffer twice? First they suffer the wrong of another person's assault. They were ripped off. Betrayed. Left out in the cold. Now must they suffer a second injury and swallow an insult to boot? They are stuck with the hurt—must they also bless the person who hurt them?

We must not preach the sublime duty of forgiving to the Simon Wiesenthals or to the Jane Graafschaps until we have chewed the cud of fairness a while. We can "believe in forgiveness only if justice is maintained and guilt is confirmed." Paul Tillich was right. When we say "forgive" we may be asking someone to commit an outrage against humankind's universal instinct for fair play.

Let us see if we *can* make a case for a fair forgiving. I suggest that we look at it from two points of view.

FORGIVING OPENS THE WAY TO A BETTER FAIRNESS

Forgiving is fair to the facts, to begin with.

Forgiving does not try to change the facts in our past. Tampering with the facts of history is faker's fancy; history is implacable. We can begin to forgive only when we refuse the soft-soaped temptation of toning down the wrong of what happened to us.

Someone has been hurt. If we are too proud to admit

that a worm like our husband or our former partner could hurt us, we may avoid the crisis for a little while. If we are too afraid of our own pain to permit ourselves to feel it fully, we may skirt the issue of forgiveness. What shoves us into crisis is our respect for the fact that we have been treated unfairly by somebody who did not have to do it. Forgiving is only for people who are fair to the wretched fact of unfair pain.

Forgiving is also fair, in a paradoxical way, to the dignity of the wrongdoer. If you believe that everything we do is determined for us ahead of time by forces beyond our control, you will never enter the forgiveness circle. If you agree that the idiots who hurt you were only victims of the fates, that they were stuck in the groove their neurotic parents set them in, that they could not help themselves, you do not need to forgive them. Pity them maybe. Retune them if possible. But do not forgive them.

You will forgive only when you dare look at people eyeball to eyeball and tell them that they are responsible for what they did. Forgiving is fair to wrongdoers because it holds them to the incriminating touchstone of their own free humanity.

But back to the heart of the matter. Is forgiving an honorable way to come to terms with the pain you feel when a responsible person stings you deeply and unfairly?

Well, what is the alternative to forgiving?

Must you freeze yourself in the unfairness of a cruel moment in the past? Do you want your private world to stand still at that wretched incident in your irreversible history? Or are you ready to find a better way? Better than what? Better than the pain of a memory glued forever to the unfair past.

But suppose you do refuse to settle for the past and you also refuse to forgive. Is there another option? Maybe revenge?

Vengeance is a passion to get even. It is a hot desire to give back as much pain as someone gave you. An eye for an eye! Fairness!

The problem with revenge is that it never gets what it wants; it never evens the score. Fairness never comes. The chain reaction set off by every act of vengeance always takes its unhindered course. It ties both the injured and the injurer to an escalator of pain. Both are stuck on the escalator as long as parity is demanded, and the escalator never stops, never lets anyone off.

Why do family feuds go on and on until everyone is dead—or gets too old and too tired to fight?

The reason is simple: no two people, no two families, ever weigh pain on the same scale. The pain a person causes me always feels heavier to me than it feels to the person who caused it. The pain I inflict on you always feels worse to you than it seems to me. Pains given and pains received never balance out. The difference between pain given and pain suffered is like the difference between climbing a hill and scampering down, it never feels the same in both directions.

If you hurt me and I retaliate in kind, I may think that I have given you only what you deserve, no more. But you will feel it as a hurt that is too great for you to accept. Your passion for fairness will force you to retaliate against me, harder this time. Then it will be my turn. And will it ever stop?

An eye for an eye becomes a leg for a leg and, eventually, a life for a life. No matter what our weapons are—words, clubs, arrows, guns, bombs, nuclear missiles—revenge locks us into an escalation of violence. Gandhi was right: if we all live by "an eye for an eye" the whole world will be blind. The only way out is forgiveness.

Forgiveness is not the alternative to revenge because it is soft and gentle; *it is a viable alternative because it is the only creative route to less unfairness*.

Forgiveness has creative power to move us away from a past moment of pain, to unshackle us from our endless chain of reactions, and to create a new situation in which both the wrongdoer and the wronged can begin a new way.

Forgiveness offers a chance at reconciliation; it is an opportunity for a life together instead of death together. Forgiveness is a miracle of the will that moves away the heavy hindrance to fellowship, a miracle that will be fulfilled when the two estranged people come together in as fair a new relationship as is possible at that time and under those circumstances.

The alternative to reconciliation is, in the end, a ceaseless process of self-destruction. The brilliant American theologian Reinhold Niebuhr saw this after World War II and said: "We must finally be reconciled with our foe, lest we both perish in the vicious circle of hatred." There must be a release from the past or we are forever grounded on its unfair pain.

Vengeance never wholly satisfies. For one thing, we are not always able to fight back. Maybe the person who hurt us is dead. Maybe we are old and weak. What is left to us then but our private truculence? We simmer in our spite, impotent to retaliate and powerless to forgive. Frustrated! Immobilized! This is not the way to make things fairer.

Vengeance mires people in a painful and unjust past. They ought to move toward a new future of fairer relationships, but the inner lust for revenge pushes them deeper into endless repetition of the old unfairness. All in the name, mind you, of fair play.

Forgiveness begins midstream in the flow of unfairness, and starts a new movement toward another fairness, imperfect fairness, to be sure, but better at least than endless perpetuation of the old unfairness. It breaks the grip that past wrong and past pain have on our minds and frees us for whatever fairer future lies amid the unknown potentialities of our tomorrows.

There is no guarantee. But forgiving is the only open door to *possibility*.

FORGIVING IS THE ONLY WAY TO BE FAIR TO
OURSELVES

When you suspect that forgiving is not fair, you worry that the people who hurt you are not getting

169

what is coming to them. But you worry, too, that you are getting a bad deal; you get hurt and do not get even. Forgiving may not seem fair to the people who must do the forgiving.

But you are not thinking clearly when you refuse to forgive on grounds that you would not be fair to yourself. Forgiving is the *only* way to be fair to yourself. Getting even is a loser's game. It is the ultimate frustration because it leaves you with more pain than you got in the first place.

Recall the pain of being wronged, the hurt of being stung, cheated, demeaned. Doesn't the memory of it fuel the fire of fury again, reheat the pain again, make it hurt again? Suppose you never forgive, suppose you feel the hurt each time your memory lights on the people who did you wrong. And suppose you have a compulsion to think of them constantly. You have become a prisoner of your past pain; you are locked into a torture chamber of your own making. Time should have left your pain behind; but you keep it alive to let it flay you over and over.

Your own memory is a replay of your hurt—a videotape within your soul that plays unending reruns of your old rendezvous with pain. You cannot switch it off. You are hooked into it like a pain junkie; you become addicted to your remembrance of pain past. You are lashed again each time your memory spins the tape. Is this fair to yourself—this *wretched justice of not forgiving?* You could not be more unfair to yourself.

The only way to heal the pain that will not heal itself is to forgive the person who hurt you. Forgiving stops the reruns of pain. Forgiving heals your memory as you change your memory's vision.

When you release the wrongdoer from the wrong, you cut a malignant tumor out of your inner life.

You set a prisoner free, but you discover that the real prisoner was yourself.

CHAPTER 19

Forgiving Is a Better Risk

Forgiving could be dangerous to your children's health. A little private forgiving now and then, for the small things, done discreetly and without a lot of fuss, will not threaten the future of human society. But if you forgive big wrongs, and forgive them indiscriminately and openly, you may doom the lives of tomorrow's innocent children.

Forgiving, then, is a serious risk.

Forgiveness, cheaply given, *is* dangerous, let us face it. If we forgive, we are likely to forget; and if we forget the horrors of the past we are likely to let them happen again in the future.

Every act of forgiving can be a nail in somebody else's coffin. If you forgive a man who rapes your sister, you may mute society's scream of outrage against rapists. If you forgive a pusher who sells your daughter cocaine, you may make it a little easier for him to get to your neighbor's daughter too. If you forgive too easily and forget too quickly, you may be turning innocent people over to predators who give not a damn about your forgiveness.

If you forgive the Nazi, it is argued, you will eventually forget the holocaust. If the Armenians forgive the Turks, their children will forget the massacres. If Ukrainian kulaks forgive Stalin, their children will forget how he starved their parents. If Cambodians forgive Pol Pot, their children will forget his massive atrocities against millions of innocent Cambodian people.

The risks of forgetting are both personal and global. Once we forgive and learn to swallow history's stinking garbage without throwing up, we condition ourselves to digest the worst the monsters of the future can force down our throats. When forgiving cures our nausea it encourages us to forget that the evil thing happened and can happen again. If we open the dike a crack, we may be in for a deluge.

After you have forgiven people, it is feared, you will begin to discover all sorts of good things about them. Concentration camp commanders were fine family men. They saw to the slaughter of little children from nine to five and went home to make soothing love to their wives in warm beds of teutonic fidelity. Mafia mobsters gun down their competition in cold blood at noon and by five are home with their children in their old-fashioned family ways. Look at both sides. Maybe the monsters of our history were not as bad as their victims thought.

Ordinary people, it is said, cannot be trusted with forgiveness. Maybe God can forgive sinners without losing his outrage at their sin. Maybe God does not bamboozle himself, maybe he knows that forgiven sinners still have enough rot in their guts to sin again. But most ordinary people let their forgiving wash out the memory and rinse away its bitter taste. They are like drunks who hate booze only as long as their hangover lasts.

As their memories dim, they turn soft. And they make their softness sound like sophisticated insight. They are all too ready, once they forgive, to plead extenuating circumstances—the burdens of history, the hard times, the poverty-drained culture, the pathological family life, the weak genes. They say it was destiny.

Beware the muddle-headed softness of the easy forgiver!

Could I put the case *against* forgiving any more strongly?

One way to reduce the risk is simply to determine not to let the future generations forget. We can tell our children the stories of the past's terrible wrongs. We can build museums to genocide, design artistic monuments to slaughter. We can vow that our children and our children's children will never be allowed not to know. We can tell it on the mountains in every generation.

We must know, however, that remembering has problems of its own. If forgetting invites repetition, remembering incites perpetuation. Memory can nurse a flame that brings hate to its boiling point, creating a pressure inside that only getting even can relieve. But you cannot get even, not ever, not if you try for a million years. So remembering takes its worst toll on the spirits of the people who suffered most.

Is there a narrows to be navigated between the rock of risky forgetting and the hard place of futile remembering?

There is a *redemptive remembering*. There is a healing way to remember the wrongs of our irreversible past, a way that can bring hope for the future along with our sorrow for the past. Redemptive remembering keeps a clear picture of the past, but it adds a new setting and shifts its focus.

No people can tell us about redemptive remembering the way the old Hebrews can. Remembering was their lifestyle. Their memories told them who they were, how they fit into the human picture, and what they were expected to do with themselves. Their future was born yesterday, and by remembering yesterday well they discovered the meaning of their today and the goal of their tomorrow.

Moses posted notice early on that the Hebrews' terrible yesterday had to be kept alive forever so people would know the meaning of what was, what is and what shall be. "Only take heed, and keep your soul diligently, lest you forget the things your eyes have seen and lest they depart from your heart all the days of your life; make them known to your children and your children's children."

No forgetting, ever. If you lose your memory, you lose your own identity. And you lose your personal stake in your people's future.

But take a closer look at what the Jews were supposed to remember. It was not the horror of their four hundred years of slavery. Though slavery was their past. Not the titantic injustice of the Pharaoh in Egypt. Though injustice was their past. They were not ordered to memorialize the evil. An astonishing feature of the post-slavery memorials is that the people are not urged to remember their misery.

What had to be remembered was the miracle of survival and renewal. What had to be remembered were not the days when God was on a leave of absence, but the day when God came back to bring them out of slavery and out of suffering.

The Passover feast was their memory day.

This day shall be a memorial day . . . and when your children shall say to you, "what do you mean by this sacrifice?" you shall say, "It is the sacrifice of the Lord's passover, for he passed over the houses of Israel in Egypt when he slew the Egyptians but spared our houses."

Release, liberation, redemption from the pain, were memorialized—not the bondage, not the wrong by itself. The monument was to the possibilities for the future, not to the horror of the past.

Redemptive remembering drives us to a better future, it does not nail us to a worse past.

When Israel remembered its own past bondage, the memory incited them to seek justice in the present. You were once strangers in a strange land; remember now to be hospitable to the stranger in your land. You were exploited by unjust masters; remember not to

174

exploit your own poor people. You were slaves once; remember to set your own slaves free. Good hopes for a better life were filaments in the light ignited by the redemptive memory of Jewish suffering.

The Christian community, too, was told from the beginning not to forget the sufferings of its founder. Remember the terrible death of Jesus until he comes again at the end of time—so early believers were commanded to do. But this remembrance is not meant to stoke the fire of resentment against the unfairness of his dying; just the opposite.

The point of remembering is to be renewed again and again by the life that rises from the aftershocks of his unfair death.

Redemptive memory is focused on love emerging from ashes, light that sheds darkness, hope that survives remembered evil.

I do not mean to underrate the chance that we will forget and that people will take advantage of our forgetting. Grace is a gamble, always. God knows. He knows what it is like to forgive and have it thrown back at him as a dare to forgive again. "Sin that grace may abound!" Why not? If forgiving is your game, and you like the exercise, we'll give you double the pleasure.

But God does take the risk, and so does anyone who ever forgives another human being.

The question is not whether forgiving is dangerous, but only whether it is a safer bet. It almost always comes down to where we get the best odds.

Forgiving is risky, but there are ways to improve the odds. One of them is to turn your remembered terrors into redemptive memories.

The risk, I believe, is worth taking.

CHAPTER 20

Forgiving Is Stronger

Passionate people are often sure that power comes only from hate and violence. We must listen to what they tell us.

Nobody in modern times has persuaded more people that violent hate is the power of the future than has Franz Fanon, the fervent Algerian psychiatrist who, in the 1960s, was the inspiration of many future black leaders. He set down his passionate philosophy in a book called *The Wretched of the Earth*—meaning all the people who live in the unfair pain of oppression and poverty. Their salvation, he believed, lies in hate's violence.

"Violence," he said, "is a cleansing force. It frees [the person who suffers unfair hurt] from his inferiority complex and from his despair and inaction; it makes him fearless and restores his self-respect."

I do not think I could find a more compelling challenge to my passion for forgiving than I find in Fanon's passion for violence.

Hate does have a feel of power to it, I admit. To a person energized by hate, forgiving feels flaccid, sapless, impotent. We feel stronger when we nourish our contempt and plot to get even. We dream up brilliant schemes for putting our enemies in their place, we pin them down in public, we make them grovel—and our vengeful dreams make us feel very strong. "The hell with you" feels a lot more macho than "I forgive you."

Hate does generate real energy. People who have been hurt and hate the villain who hurt them experience a surge of power inside. American prisoners, survivers of Bataan, forced on their terrible death march, prodded by the enemies' bayonets, fed rotten food, given no reason to hope for escape or survival, tell us that it was their hate that gave them the power to make it out alive.

But we must bring the matter down to where ordinary people live. Take Marcie Rozen, for instance. Marcie was deserted by her husband, left without money, without skills for the marketplace, without self-esteem, feeling unloved and unlovable. Ask her what helped her most to get out of the sinking sand of her despair, into school to train for a job, into the marketplace to find one, and, from there, into success at the job she found. Marcie will tell you: "I wanted to show the louse he couldn't hurt me. Hate gave me strength."

What does a forgiver have to say to Marcie's testimony?

This: hate gives instant energy, but it runs dry after the suffering stops. Hate can keep us going while we feel battered, but the drive dies down as time goes on after the ordeal is over. And then hate turns its power against the hater. It saps the energy of the soul, leaving it weaker than before, too weak to create a better life beyond the pain.

Hate is for emergencies, like a fast battery charge; it is a quick fix like heroin. As a long-term energizer, it is unreliable. And in the end it kills.

Hate-power is especially superficial when it is generated by our *fear* of weakness. Let me share a typical little story to show what I mean.

Mark Zwaak thinks of his wife, Karen, as an efficient, aggressive, domineering woman, while he sees himself as an ineffective, timid, submissive man. Karen goads Mark a lot; she wants him to take charge of the children, make decisions, face up to the mechanic who rips him off, get ahead in his job, and generally stop letting people push him around. Mark is miserable; he hates himself for being the weak member of the partnership.

One night, at a party with friends, overextended on Chablis, Karen laughingly said that she despised Mark for being a mama's boy who had never grown up. The icy meanness of Karen's jibe froze Mark's feelings into a hard block of hate. His wilted shame became an erection of rage. When they got home Mark stepped on the throttle of his humiliated ego and screamed: "For this, I will never forgive you, never!"

And he did not forgive. His hate became his secret pet; he succored it, nourished it, fondled it, and let it roam the ranges of his soul. His hate felt to him like a generator of inner power.

But his hate was only surface strength. Beneath his hate, he still suspected that Karen had him sized up right; he really was weak, impotent, ineffective. His hate was a cover for the weakness he dared not face.

Karen wasn't fooled; she understood that Mark's powerful hate was only a mask for his weakness, the only disguise he could find. She knew Mark.

But she hardly knew herself at all. She closed her eyes to the fact that her own cocky toughness was a well-tuned instrument for keeping her own weakness under control. Karen was scared of a legion of secret demons flitting inside of her soul, and she needed strength from Mark so that he could be her crutch. But Mark was not strong enough, so she played the tiresome game of being stronger than he was in order to hide her weakness.

But Karen learned. It took a near nervous collapse to teach her that we never win the game of being only strong and never weak. Through counsel and through pain, she came to terms with being weak, with being afraid, with being needy. So she threw away the mark of her jaunty self-confidence.

When she finally came to terms with being needy she found a truer strength. For instance, she found the courage to tell Mark how weak and how afraid she really was, and how cruel she had been when she demanded that Mark never be weak. She knew now that strength comes only in weakness. Why not be weak together?

The happy ending began when Mark agreed to join Karen in a counseling program that aimed, not at getting strong, but at helping them to accept their fragile, weak, human selves. It took tears, a river of tears, to wash away the crazy conviction that in order to be strong he was not allowed to be weak. But he shed the tears, and they washed away his illusion.

As he learned that strength is given to us only in a package of weakness, Mark became strong enough to drop his mask of manly hate. Why not? A person who is not ashamed of being weak does not need the disguise.

The notion that hate is strong and forgiving is weak is a fallacy fabricated of a phony notion of strength. It pits strength against weakness as if we have to be one or the other, either strong *or* weak. And so, like a bad movie, it presents life in blacks and whites the way life seldom is. We are never *either* strong *or* weak; we are always *both* strong *and* weak. And in that combination we find our humanness.

Forgiving is a creative way to be weak and, therewith, a most human way to be strong.

Let us go on to *name* some of its strengths.

FORGIVING IS REALISM

Forgiving comes equipped with the toughness of realism. To be able to forgive we must have the guts to look hard at the wrongness, the horridness, the sheer wickedness of what somebody did to us. We cannot camouflage; we cannot excuse; we cannot ignore. We eye the evil face to face and we call it what it is. Only realists can be forgivers.

One prime reason why some people cannot forgive is their fear of reality. Parents miss chances to forgive their children because they are afraid to face the facts. A mother has a sixth sense that her son is stealing money from her. He needs money to buy drugs for himself and gas for his van; but he has lost his job. So he pilfers at home. She misses a ten-dollar bill here, a twenty there, out of her purse and out of her dresser drawer. He leaves hints behind, clear enough to give himself away. She knows; but she refuses to acknowledge what she knows. She stuffs her knowledge safely into her subconscious bag of unpleasant facts. She closes her eyes and she avoids the crisis of forgiving.

Self-deception is a lot easier than forgiving. But it has no payoff in healing.

Forgiving begins with the power to shake off deception and deal with reality.

FORGIVING IS CONFRONTATION

The strength of forgiving is seen most clearly whenever it is born of confrontation. We cannot completely forgive anyone whom we do not—one way or the other—face up to and say: "You did me wrong and I hate you for it."

Liz Bentley is an assistant professor of biology at a university in California. She is not a scholar, but she is a good teacher. She was up for promotion and the chairman of her department promised that he would persuade the dean to promote her on the basis of her work in the classroom. Liz counted on him.

As it turned out the dean called her in and told her that she was not going to get a promotion. And he advised her to begin applying for other jobs.

She felt like a hopeless failure at first, and was just beginning to climb out of her slough when a gossipy colleague let it slip that her chairman had not recommended her at all, had in fact pooh-poohed her performance as a teacher.

Liz was betrayed by the man who promised to be

her advocate. She had been bitten from behind by an academic jackal. She hated him.

She also needed a recommendation from him. So, for a while, she played games, acting as if she believed him when he told her how sorry he was that not even his strong support for her could convince the dean. And she went home each night and vomited.

But Liz could not keep her dialogue of duplicity going for long. She had to stop lying to the chairman and force him to stop lying to her. She would confront him, and if she had to she would flush his recommendation down the toilet. She met him at the coffee urn, drew him aside, looked him in the eye, and said: "Jack, I know you threw me down the shaft and I hate you for it." The chairman lied again and walked away.

Liz now began to feel the power she needed to forgive the man. She knew it would not be easy; she was not sure whether she could do it at all. But having risen in power, she felt strong enough to be weak enough to forgive. So, in her mind, she stripped his jackal's hide and saw him as the poor, weak person he was beneath it.

And in her decision to forgive she was set free. She went to bed without vomiting; she put away the Valium. Now she knew that whatever academic road she walked, she would walk it as a free woman.

FORGIVING IS FREEDOM

Nobody can make you forgive.

Only a free person can choose to live with an uneven score. Only free people can choose to start over with someone who has hurt them. Only a free person can live with accounts unsettled. Only a free person can heal the memory of hurt and hate.

When you forgive another person you are surprised at your own freedom to do what you did. All the king's armies could not have forced you to do it. You forgive

181

in freedom and then move on to greater freedom. Freedom is strength; you know you have it when you have the power to forgive.

FORGIVING IS LOVE'S ULTIMATE POWER

Love is the power behind forgiveness.

But it does not work the way a lot of people suppose.

Love is not a soft and fuzzy sentiment that lets people get away with almost everything, no matter what they do to us. Love does not make us pushovers for people who hurt us unfairly.

Love forgives, but only because love is powerful.

Love has two ingredients that make it strong. One ingredient is respect. The other is *commitment*.

On the one hand, these two qualities make us vulnerable enough to need to forgive. On the other hand, they give us power to do the forgiving we need to do.

First, consider love's power to give you respect for yourself.

If you love yourself truly, you will respect yourself truly. And it is precisely your self-respect that gets you into situations where you are challenged to forgive.

When you respect yourself, you set limits to the abuse that you can accept from thoughtless or cruel people, even if you love them. Some pain will be unacceptable to you for the simple reason that you have too much dignity to deserve it. You will not accept disloyalty from friends you trust, or betrayals from spouses you love, or abuse from children you care for. Such hurts go beyond the limits that a self-respecting person allows.

Love is too powerful to let you lump all the blame for your pain on yourself, as if it must always be your fault when your father deprives you of love, or your spouse has an affair, or your children throw away your values. Love does not let you blame yourself falsely for long. Sometimes it reaches down into the reservoir of your nobility and says: "No more, I have too much self-respect to put up with any more."

When love gives you back your self-respect, and you refuse to take it anymore, you will have to make a decision about forgiveness.

Will you glue yourself to the painful memory of the hurt you didn't deserve? Will you roll it around your memories, savor its bitter taste, squeeze the last ounce of crazy-making pleasure you can get out of your pain? Or will you, in self-respect, forgive and set yourself free?

The same self-respecting love that gets you into the *crisis of forgiving* has the power to move you into the *place of self-healing.*

Love will not let you lock yourself in the prison cell of your bitter memories. It will not permit you the demeaning misery of wallowing in yesterday's pain. Your love for yourself will generate enough energy, finally, to say: "I have had enough; I am not going to put myself down by letting somebody's low blow keep hurting me forever." And so you begin forgiving.

Now you can reverse your focus and point your love toward the people who hurt you. Love enables you to respect them too, no matter how mean, cruel, or terribly unfair they were.

The highest respect you can show people is to let them take responsibility for their own actions. Love has this power, the power to let people be responsible for hurting us.

Love does *not* forever cover up for people, it does *not* forever find excuses for them, or protect them. I know a man whose wife is an alcoholic, and who, when she drinks, is abusive and cutting. She hurts him very deeply. But he does not dare tell her to get help for herself, nor does he dare leave her on her own to decide whether she wants to get help, and he certainly will not get out of the house to protect himself. He says he loves her too much. But he does not love her with the powerful love of respect; he does not give her the simplest respect of letting her take responsibility for herself.

When we really love people with respect, we let them be accountable for what they do to us. And then we face the crisis of forgiving.

But now comes the marvelous turnabout. Again, just as love gets us into the crisis, love gives us the power to get out of it.

Love respects people as genuine human beings, even after they have treated you like dirt. People who hurt you so badly are not just lumps of degenerate corruption; they are complex people with more to them than meanness and craziness. They have the potential to become better people, truer people, than they were when they stung you. Respect for them will help you to see the *person* behind the rat. And this respect can stimulate you to move in the direction of forgiveness.

So much, then, for love's power to respect yourself and the person who hurt you.

Now let us go on to the second ingredient in the power of love, *love's power to risk a commitment*.

True love dares to commit itself to someone, and therein lies both its vulnerability and its power.

When you commit yourself you reach out into a future you cannot control and you make an appointment to be there with someone you love. You pledge yourself to be there with them no matter what the circumstances are. And in committing yourself to people, you expect them to commit themselves to you.

But what a risk it is to trust anyone's commitment, not least your own. I am not surprised that people break their commitments; what amazes me is that we have the courage to make them in the first place. Commitments make us very vulnerable.

If you do not dare to risk forgiving, all you have to do is avoid commitments. You can keep your options open, your bags packed, so you can slip out into greener pastures whenever you are not getting a good payoff on your relationship. You can run away from pain, run quickly and leave others to pick up the pieces for you. Or you can become an urban hermit and never allow yourself to get involved with anyone beyond what it takes to get along on the job. If you can avoid any of love's commitments, you can live a long time without ever having to forgive.

But anyone whose love dares to commit him is a candidate for forgiving. For when love commits you, it opens you up to hurts from people who go back on their commitments. And when you get hurt, as most of us do, you either walk onstage to dance to the music of forgiveness or stew backstage in your own depressing pain.

But now comes the turnabout again. The very love that dares to be vulnerable by making a commitment has power to heal you of the pain that commitments bring.

Committed love does not say "finish" before the last act is played out. It gives us the strength to tough out bad times in the hope of better times. Committed love does not throw in the towel before the fight is really over. It holds on. And while it holds, it energizes, it gives you strength to keep the door open for the day when a new beginning may be possible.

I have been saying that, over the long run, love's power to forgive is stronger than hate's power to get even. I admit that hate gives a temporary power for surviving today's brutality and it has a short-term power to move us into tough action for tomorrow. But hate lacks staying power to create a fairer future beyond revenge.

It is forgiveness that supplies the healing stream of the long-term tomorrows. For long distance, forgiving is stronger than hate.

CHAPTER 21

Forgiving Fits Faulty People

There is a good guy and a bad guy in every forgiving crisis. Someone has hurt someone else, wrongly and deeply; one person needs to forgive and another needs to be forgiven.

But when we look at the *whole* picture, we always discover that those who get hurt probably need to be forgiven, too, by somebody. And if they need forgiveness, they have extra reason to forgive those who hurt them.

We always feel like innocent lambs when someone hurts us unfairly. But we are never as pure as we feel. I may have been betrayed, cheated, maligned, and in several other ways badly abused, and feel as if I am as benign as a shorn sheep. But being abused does not make me a good person. As Reinhold Neibuhr kept telling us years ago: "There is a labyrinth of motives in every heart; and every action, both good and evil, is the consequence of a complicated debate and tension within the soul." We are all too complex to be pure.

Moreover, we are seldom *merely* sinned against. We often contribute to our own vulnerability. We set ourselves up for hurt. Sometimes we invite pain, not because we love somebody too much, but because we are too stupid. Maybe we contribute to our being ripped-off because we are too lazy to look hard before we leap into a deal. Maybe we contribute to our spouse's infidelity by our unfeeling ignorance of their needs and desires. Maybe we contribute to our children's rebellion by our cold judgments and hot tempers. Surely, we know at least this much, that even if we are the *hurt* party, we are seldom a completely *innocent* party.

Our virtue is always compromised; we are never as innocent as we feel when we taste our early hate for a person who hurt us.

Our own faults, therefore, reduce the gap between us and whoever did us wrong. We do not toss our forgiving down from the peak of a holy mountain; we are in the valley with those who hurt us.

Aleksandr Solzhenitsyn, the novelist who was kicked out of Russia because he could not keep his mouth shut about the truth, and now lives and works in the United States, tells, in *The Gulag Archipelago,* about his friendship with an army officer during World War II. He felt then that he and his friend were almost completely alike; they had the same convictions, the same hopes, and the same feelings about everything.

But after the war, their destinies took them in opposite directions.

Solzhenitsyn was thrown into prison with uncounted other innocent Russians, gobbled into the unfathomable Soviet gulag machinery. He survived on a daily regimen of courage.

But what happened to his friend? He became one of the interrogators who forced confessions out of innocent people by methods so vicious that one cringes to read of them.

So we have two friends who loved each other, who felt as if they came out of the same mold, and who were sure that they would live out their lives in the same useful way. But one becomes his generation's eloquent example of human courage. The other becomes a willing agent in an insane network of human brutality.

Solzhenitsyn wondered how he and his friend could have turned out so differently from each other. But one thing he would not believe. He would not believe that he was a totally good person and his friend was a totally evil person. Solzhenitsyn knew himself too well.

So we find him saying that, if he had been in the wrong place, under the wrong teachers, in the wrong circumstance, he could have ended up exactly as his friend did.

Consider what he says while he wonders about the difference between him and his former friend:

> If only there were vile people . . . committing evil deeds, and it were only necessary to separate them from the rest of us and destroy them. But the line dividing good and evil cuts through the heart of every human being. And who is willing to destroy a piece of his own heart?
>
> During the life of any heart this line keeps changing place; sometimes it is squeezed one way by exuberant evil and sometimes it shifts to allow enough space for good to flourish. One and the same human being is, at various ages, under various circumstances, a totally different human being. At times he is close to being a devil, at times to sainthood. But his name doesn't change, and to that name we ascribe the whole lot, good and evil.

These, mind you, are the words of a man whose own character has come, in our time, to incarnate simple human courage and uncorrupted integrity.

I have a troubling habit of putting myself in the shoes of people who do wrong. When I read a true story about a villain who does great harm to people, I wonder what I might have done had I been subject to the same influences as he was. Take slaveholders for instance, including those who were cruelest to their slaves. What if I had been a Georgia plantation owner? Would I have had the moral sense to see how evil slavery was? I don't know for sure, but I suspect I would have done what most other white people did then.

When I am counseling a man who admits to having

188

hurt someone he loved, I put myself in his place and wonder whether I would have done all that much better than he did. And I know in my heart that I may well have done no better.

I do not think I am being morbid. I think that I am reminding myself that much of my apparent virtue is nothing but good luck and the grace of God. Put me in other circumstances, where to be honest or courageous requires a very high price, and I could not guarantee anyone that I would be a hero.

We are all a mixed breed. We have both Jezebel and the Virgin Mary inside our souls—all of us—and they are never far apart. So who are *we* to believe that we are too innocent to forgive the person who is guilty of hurting us?

Forgiving fits faulty folk. And we are all faulty. The best of us belong to that catholic club where nobody dares throw the first stone. For us to forgive others, then, has a certain congruity about it, a kind of fittingness, for the mixed bag of vice and virtue that we all are.

All this explains why Jesus was so tough on sinners who refused to forgive other sinners. He saw the laughable incongruity of people who need to be forgiven a lot turning their backs on people who need a little forgiving from them.

He tells a story about a palace servant who was forgiven a large debt; his king forgave him a debt of ten thousand talents, a sum it would take fifteen years to pay off in labor. After he was forgiven this enormous debt, the servant met a man who owed him a mere hundred denarii, a sum that could be worked off in a day; the king's servant demanded every denarius. When the king heard, he summoned the servant, took back his forgiveness, and slapped him into servitude to work off the ten thousand talents to the last denarius.

The story is about God and us. If we act like the unforgiving servant, God will act like the king.

Jesus grabs the hardest trick in the bag—forgiving— and says we have to perform it or we are out in the cold, way out, in the boondocks of the unforgiven. He makes us feel like the miller's daughter who was told that if she didn't spin gold out of a pile of straw before morning, she would lose her head. And no Rumpelstiltskin is going to come and spin forgiving out of our straw hearts. But why is Jesus so tough on us?

He is tough because the incongruity of sinners refusing to forgive sinners boggles God's mind. He cannot cope with it; there is no honest way to put up with it.

So he says: if you want forgiving from God and you cannot forgive someone who needs a little forgiving from you, forget about the forgiveness you want. Take away the eloquence of King James English and you get Jesus saying something like this: if you refuse to forgive other people when you expect to be forgiven, you can go to hell.

The gift of being forgiven and love's power to forgive are like yin and yang. Each needs the other to exist. To receive the gift without using the power is absurd; it is like exhaling without inhaling or like walking without moving your legs.

It is really a question of style. How do you *usually* respond to people who hurt you? Do you *always* go for the jugular? Do you plan revenge *every time* someone treats you badly? Is getting even a way of life? If you *never* even *want* to forgive, *never* even *try* to remove a hateful memory and restore a loving relationship, you are in a lot of trouble.

If you are *trying* to forgive; even if you manage forgiving in fits and starts, if you forgive today, hate again tomorrow, and have to forgive again the day after, you are a forgiver. Most of us are amateurs, bungling duffers sometimes. So what? In this game nobody is an expert. We are all beginners.

Postlude

We have seen the unpredictable, outrageous, and creative thing we do when we forgive another human being.

We reverse the flow of seemingly irreversible history . . . of our own history . . . of our private painful history. We reverse the flow of pain that began in the past when someone hurt us, a flow that filters into our present to wound our memory and poison our future. We heal ourselves.

It is utterly *unpredictable;* no one could suspect, in the nature of things, in the natural cause and effect of things, that anyone should ever forgive.

We perform a miracle that hardly anyone notices.

We do it alone; other people can help us, but when we finally do it, we perform the miracle in the private place of our inner selves.

We do it silently, no one can record our miracle on tape.

We do it invisibly, no one can record our miracle on film.

We do it freely, no one can ever trick us into forgiving someone.

It is *outrageous:* when we do it we commit an outrage against the strict morality that will not rest with anything short of an even score.

It is *creative:* when we forgive we come as close as any human being can to the essentially divine act of creation. For we create a new beginning out of past pain that never had a right to exist in the first place. We create healing for the future by changing a past that had no possibility in it for anything but sickness and death.

When we forgive we ride the crest of love's cosmic wave; we walk in stride with God.

And we heal the hurt we never deserved.